D1319910

Married Men and Magic Tricks: John Updike's Erotic Heroes

Elizabeth Tallent

Creative Arts Book Company

For information please address:
Creative Arts Book Company,
833 Bancroft Way
Berkeley, CA 94710.
This is number five in the Creative Arts
Modern Authors Monograph Series.

The cover painting, "Eve Tempted by the Serpent," c. 1530,
by Lucas Cranach, The Elder, is used by kind permission of
The Art Institute of Chicago.

The frontispiece photograph of John Updike is © 1981 by
Ellen Dahlberg and is used by permission of Ellen Dahlberg.

Grateful acknowledgment is made to the following for
permission to reprint previously published material:
W. W. Norton & Company, Inc.: two lines from *Sphere: The
Form of a Motion*, by A. R. Ammons, Copyright © 1974,
Library of Congress Catalogue Card No. PS 3501 M6S6.

Library of Congress Catalogue Card No. 81-71726.
ISBN 0-916870-45-6 (clothbound)
ISBN 0-916870-46-4 (paperbound)

Design: Michael Patrick Cronan
Creative Arts books are published by Donald S. Ellis

Manufactured in the United States of America.

this book is for Bar

I reasoned thus: just as the paper is the basis for the marks upon it, might not events be contingent upon a never-expressed (because featureless) ground? Is the true marvel of Sunday skaters the pattern of their pirouettes or the fact that they are silently upheld?

—John Updike

Contents

Preface

A PREFACE OUGHT TO BE A SHY THING, BONY AND rather cool, like a handshake: it ought to give you a sense that what follows is going to go quickly and well. But I read Updike first for love, on buses, or when I had the flu, and a handshake seems insufficient. I am reluctant to banish my first infatuation to the distinctly unwistful tone of voice appropriate to criticism. Exegesis looks most profound in the margins of paperback books that still carry the haughty incense of swimming pool chlorine; so *Couples* is still for me a spring book—read on bleachers while a boy picked clotted grass from his baseball cleats. *The Centaur* has a perplexed, creaking heartbeat, as of oars in the locks of an old green rowboat slowly crossing a lake. *Marry Me* is wintry, and was at first a library book, one page blotted with jam. Henry Bech observes: "My books are human transactions—flirtations, quarrels." I know which these books have been, for me.

If this thread is clearly idosyncratic, I would still like to believe it reliable, and affection as good a way into the maze as any other. I have been drawn toward whatever seemed to me, within Updike's fiction, most strikingly curious or beautiful or lively, and I have often valued impulse over consistency, so that this work cannot claim to be either methodical or comprehensive. I have even slighted books that I admired—*The Coup*, for one, but *The Centaur's* exclusion was the more reluctant—because of considerations of length. Still, it is my hope that—as in the game children play, connecting numbered dots with pencil strokes—the shape of the animal will emerge complete, no matter how brief and haphazard-seeming the original lines.

I wish to thank Thomas Farber for his continuing insight and patience, Christian McEwen for the care and precision of her reading, and Andrew Wylie for his steadfast encouragement.

—Elizabeth Tallent

Introduction

JOHN UPDIKE WISHES TO LEAVE NO STONE IN EDEN unturned. His heroes often have the bewildered expectancy, the new-minted manners and uneven sexual proclivities of Adam; his heroines are usually a little skeptical and remote, as if they are used to being blamed for things that are not entirely their fault. The quality of their housekeeping, and the shapes of their feet, are observed as closely as if these were remarkable attributes in any creature—and so they may have seemed, to Adam.

"A man without a wife/is like a turtle without a shell," wrote Robert Lowell. Updike himself has said that he would choose, if he could be any animal, to become a turtle. "Turtles live quite long and can retreat immediately, and live very close to the grass, the smell of which I've always liked." (*Picked-Up Pieces*: 499) The desire for retreat, and the equal and opposite yearning for erotic risk, provide the primary tensions for much of Updike's fiction. His heroes have a way of seeming almost physiologically bereft in bachelorhood. They seem more unwifed than single. The short stories in *Problems* are documents, not only of enormous emotional dislocation, but of a sort of aggrieved pragmaticism. Updike observed that, following his own divorce, "I found living alone much harder work, more time misspent on elemental matters than I do in marriage." (*John Callaway Interviews*: 12) Updike's heroes have taken on the shapes of the various interiors they have inhabited, the press of domesticity, the imprint of the carapace. Divorce is an extreme of exposure second only to death.

The way these heroes handle their vulnerability is at once absurd and alarming; as a certain king turned everything he touched into gold, so Updike's heroes turn the women they sleep with into wives. This—like the habit of the king—begins to have its drawbacks. Even Rabbit Angstrom, at his most questing and changeable in *Rabbit, Run*, cannot escape this pattern when he treats a prostitute with such troubled gentleness that she comes to seem his wife. Piet Hanema desires nothing less than to be "the world's husband." Jerry Conant's cruel fault, his lover observes, "was that he acted like a husband. She had never had a husband before. It seemed to her that she had been married ten years to a man who wanted only to be her lover, keeping between them the distance that lovers must cross."(*Marry Me*: 21) So inevitably— so expertly, even—are Updike's heroes fitted for the role of husband that they displace even the men to whom their mistresses are married. Marriage, it seems, does not guarantee that a man will take the part of husband. Husbanding is more mysterious than that—it can exist where marriage does not, and disappear where it does. To this mysterious act Updike's heroes are deeply drawn. They find brides everywhere; they don't take lovers, they take adumbrations of future wives. "I made you and the sun and the stars," Rabbit tells his prositute-love, Ruth. "I made you bloom."

"Oh you're a wonder," she says, and in spite of the flatness of her voice she is signalling a truth: he *is* a wonder. Rabbit, in his guise of Adam, has confiscated some of God's sleight of hand, and donated not only a single utilitarian rib but also an invaluable element of ease and delight to Eve's psyche. Newly loved, in Updike's work, means newly invented. His heroes are as adept at this first burnishing—the blooming of brand-new lovers—as they are heavy-handed and disparaging with their wives, who seem, in consequence, to darken, thicken, and diminish. Here are two women, one in the early stages of an affair with an Updike protagonist, and the other near the end of a long and complex marriage:

> In the months that unfolded from this, it had been his pleasure to see her stare relax. Her body gathered softness under his; late one night, after yet another party, his wife, lying beside him in the pre-dawn darkness of her ignorance, had remarked, with the cool, fair appraisal of a rival woman, how beautiful she—*she*, the other—had become, and he had felt, half dreaming in the warm bed he had betrayed, justified. Her laugh no longer flashed out so hungrily, and her eyes, brimming with the secret he and she had made, deepened and seemed to rejoin the girlishness that had lingered in the other features of her face. Seeing her across a room standing swathed in the beauty he had given her, he felt a creator's, a father's, pride. ("The Stare," in *The Music School*: 60)

> She was growing older; the skin of her face, as she bowed her head to cry, puckered and dripped in little dry points below her eyes, at the corners of her mouth. He was moved, as by beauty. Unthinkingly, she had clasped her hands in her lap, her hands white against the black flannel skirt; with that yoga-performing flexibility of hers, that age had not yet taken from her, she had made herself compact, into a grieving ball, as if about to be shot from a cannon. ("Divorcing: A Fragment," from *Too Far to Go*: 232-233)

One woman's eyes are "brimming," while the other's, even weeping, seem adamantly dry. One is a relaxed young Eve, the other a sort of aging acrobat about to be robbed, not only of her marriage, but even of her original suppleness. The curious image of being shot from a cannon suggests how alien a trick the process of divorce is, for her, and how passive she is, confronted with such domestic violence. For the hero to be moved "as by beauty" is to cruelly echo his earlier response, the reaction to beauty itself. Because he is so powerful—his vigilance causes one woman to become beautiful, his indifference causes another to stiffen and grieve—each motion of his attention is freighted with responsibility. Part of the resourcefulness of a magician lies in his ability to channel magic properly, to allocate wonders. Updike's heroes seem ill-acquainted with this technique. "She'll live," Jerry Conant's lover assures him, of the wife Jerry wishes to leave, and he replies, "I wish I was sure of that. If only there was some decent man who I know would marry her and take care of her—but every man we know, compared to me, is a clunk. Really. I'm not conceited, but that's a fact." (*Marry Me*: 59) Thomas Marshfield, in *A Month of Sundays*, believes that no woman can be happy without him; he sleeps with his parishoners out of a sense of ritualized obligation, purely for their own good. "In a sense you are my first *companion*," Foxy tells her lover Piet in *Couples*, thereby reducing her husband, already a shadowy presence, to a malleable ghost. In an odd way it is as if these women had never *seen* a man before. They have certainly slept with, and even married, someone other than the hero himself, but these predecessors seem little more than outlines about whose details the women seem uncertain. Heroes alone, in Updike's work, are truly solid, truly capable of altering the fixed course of a woman's life, truly able to pose the erotic dilemma in all its formidably rich dimensions.

Jacques Dopagne once wrote that for the painter Magritte nakedness was "an ontological attribute of woman. Hardly erotic at all, often entirely chaste, she seems to pose in all her hieratic beauty, her gestures minimal." I find a similar stasis—not erotic, and rather coolly hieratic—in Updike's descriptions of his heroes' wives. Their gestures, like Joan Maple's clasped hands, tend to be minimal, constricted, meek even in protest. In another story, "Nakedness," Joan Maple "halts in the pose of Michelangelo's slave, of Munch's madonna, of Ingres' urnbearer . . . ." (*Too Far to Go*: 191), all positions of forbearance, all sorrowing. In contrast, a lover is likely to be described as wide, with something extravagant, expansive, or even sweepingly awkward in her stance. "God, you looked great," Jerry tells his lover, "rolling along with that farm-girl gait, your big feet wobbling away in heels." (*Marry Me*: 33) Women in love can afford to be clumsy; wives manifest loss by the progessive impoverishment, not only of their bodies, but of their movements. The implication is that in disorder lies possibility, and that the lover is, for the hero, defined by the clumsily vivid intersection of possibilities. In the beginning she should seem pliant, rich, even bulky, with something unshaped about her, an unfinishedness that corresponds to the hero's ambition. Jerry tells his lover: "I want to *shape* you, to make you all over again. I feel I could. I don't feel this with Ruth [his wife]. Somehow, she's formed, and the best kind of life I can live with her will be lived in"—his finger illustrated the word in the air—"parallel." (*Marry Me*: 49)

Parallel lives disappoint; they suggest a fixity, a parity, that is dulling to the spirit. Convergence requires movement—the tenuous nearing, the precarious pulling away—that can try a hero's mettle, test the depth of his ingeniousness, the dare inherent in "I feel I could." In another context, the melee-like interview that concludes the collection *Picked-Up Pieces*, Updike has described his own sensation that "the people we meet are guises, and do conceal something mythic, perhaps prototypes or longings in our own minds. We love some women more than others by predetermination, it seems to me."

If the love of certain women is predetermined, the consequences of that love are not, or the life of an Updike hero would be far easier. A hero must recognize the unknowns—the x of erotic risk, the y of domestic calm—and comprehend the equation by which they are covertly, inevitably, linked. Equations exist, or can be devised, to match any sort of sexual enigma, but often the very terms in which the problem is cast balk its clear resolution.

> "Decide, please," Ruth pleaded. "We'll all survive, just do what you want and stop caring about us."
> "I can't," he said. "What I want is too tied up with how it affects everybody else. It's like one of those equations with nothing but variables. I can't solve it. I can't solve it." (*Marry Me*: 168)

> . . . During the night, *A*, though sleeping with *B*, dreams of *C*. *C* stands at the furthest extremity or (if the image is considered two-dimensionally) the apogee of a curved driveway, perhaps a dream-refraction of the driveway of the house that had once been their shared home. Her figure, although small in the perspective, is vivid, clad in a tomato-red summer dress; her head is thrown back, her hands are on her hips, and her legs have taken a wide, confident stance. She is flaunting herself, perhaps laughing; his impression is of intense female vitality, his emotion of longing. He awakes troubled. The sleep of *B* beside him is not disturbed; she rests in the certainty that *A* loves her. Indeed, he has left *C* for her, to prove it.
> PROBLEM: Which has he more profoundly betrayed, *B* or *C*? ("Problems," in *Problems*: 150)

The phrase "more profoundly betrayed" admits of no solution, no discernable way to reduce the almost overwhelming tensions of betrayal and attraction. It locks the problem, as Jerry Conant said, into a dialectic composed entirely of variables. This stubborn refusal to slight complexity is unique to Updike's fiction; very rarely has the ordinary texture of life been shown to consist of such opaque stuff. Intractable, ineluctable, riddling—

those are the qualities of emotion that draw Updike's eye, and daunt his heroes. Release glimmers distantly. Indeed, if any word in the language can be said to belong exclusively to one writer, then this grave, apprehensive, schoolchild-like noun, "problems," belongs to Updike. He gives it the definitive shading in the short story "Solitaire." "Problems to which there is any solution at all, no matter how difficult or complex, are not really problems. . . . Night by night, lying awake, he had digested the embarrassments, the displacements, the disappointments, the reprimands and lectures and appeals that were certain; one by one he had made the impossibilities possible. At last he had stripped the problem to its two white poles, the two women." (*Museums and Women*: 81) Into this brief catalogue an enormity of grief is compressed: "the embarrassments, the displacements, the disappointments, the reprimands and lectures and appeals . . ." Updike's later fiction will not neglect these disappointments; they show plainly through the fabric of *Too Far to Go* and *Problems*. But in these middle stories, the stories of perplexity, love seems to lie in the ability to equivocate. As long as he equivocates, a hero remains, in one sense at least, faithful to his wife, true to the depth of complexity as he encounters it.

This insistence on questioning, equivocation, and self-reproach is central to Updike's portrayal of sexual love. His heroes are reasonable men confronting the sheer unreasonableness of their own hearts. They possess to a remarkable degree the willingness to bog down, to trip over erotic difficulties, to demonstrate what Keats defined as negative capability, "being in uncertainties, mysteries, doubts, without any irritable reaching after fact and reason." In fact, a sort of unreasoning vulnerability seems necessary before love can exist at all.

His brain—that impatient organ, which deals, with the speed of light, in essences and abstractions—opted to love her perhaps too early, before his heart—that plodder, that

> problem-learner—had had time to collect quirks and spiritual snapshots, to survey those faults and ledges of the not-quite-expected where affection can silt and accumulate. (*Problems*: 175)

Clearly, love belongs to the problem-learner, the plodder, rather than to the impatient brain; in matters where you are asked to choose between a tortoise and a hare, it is wise to bet on the tortoise.

So the place of a man, between innocence and alarmed knowledge, is as precarious as it ever was in Eden. "There are no stubborn truths," John Cheever once said in a *Paris Review* interview, and Updike would seem to agree, for throughout his work certainties are fragile and costly, problems dimestore-cheap and enduring. The single great domestic truth accessible to nearly all of Updike's characters is marriage; the single great uncertainty is posed by the possibility of adultery. The tension between the two polarities works to assure married men that they are alive, that existence is awesomely variable, that risk is plentiful. "Ruth disliked, religiously, the satisfaction [her unfaithful husband] took in being divided, confirming thereby the split between body and soul that alone can save men from extinction." (*Marry Me*: 178) Nothing about this sentence is inadvertent: not the flinty adverb "religiously" applied to the wife's disliking; not the absence of "as if" (*as if* confirming the split between body and soul); and not the curiously severe sound of "that *alone* can save men from extinction." Men, in Updike's fiction, tend to be hauntingly well-acquainted with the possibility of extinction. According to this coda, adultery is more than a way of proving you are alive; it becomes a way of proving you will never die.

Renunciation of the mistress can seal this split, mending the breach between body and soul but extinguishing hope in the process. This is the reason for the sad, discordant note on which the story "Museums and Women" ends: ". . . it appeared to me now that I was condemned, in my search for the radiance that had faded behind me, to enter more and more museums, and to be a little less exalted by each new entrance, and a little more quickly disenchanted by the familiar contents beyond." (*Museums and Women*: 17) Mendedness, wholeness, and the recovery of equilibrium are not things that Updike values highly. He has said that "a person who has what he wants, a satisfied person, a content person, ceases to be a person. Unfallen Adam is an ape. Yes, I guess I do feel that. I feel that to be a person is to be in a situation of tension, to be in a dialectical situation. A truly adjusted person is not a person at all—just an animal with clothes on." (*Picked-Up Pieces*: 485) If that is so, then there are not very many animals-with-clothes-on in Updike's work. His men and women are caught in situations of enormous tension, and very few of them could be said to be "truly adjusted" for more than a paragraph or two.

These ancient alternatives—fidelity and adultery—parallel the choices once offered in Eden. The original existence was innocent, faithful, and unperplexed; its alternative was framed by the crucial possibility of knowledge. Without knowledge, Eden would have been simply one more rain forest, beautiful but not baffling. When the serpent describes the consequences of eating the fruit to Eve, he says, "You will not die. For God knows that when you eat of it your eyes will be opened, and you will be like God, knowing good and evil." When Eve considers the tree, she finds it "a delight to the eyes." This part of the narrative—in essence a seduction—is cast in strongly visual terms. Like the tree, a lover is "a delight to the eyes." Through infidelity, a hero's eyes are opened to delight. It *is* possible to live without certain sorts of knowledge, to endure within the confines of the threatened habitat which is human commitment. But would anyone be a hero if he abided by commandment rather than curiosity? Updike appears to believe not. When Foxy Whitman in *Couples* confronts Piet, the hero, with the seriousness of what has happened between them, he argues subtly, yet conclusively, for risk:

> "I remember it very clearly. How we moved from room to room, the cat jumping on the bed. It's all so silly, isn't it? Adultery. It's so much *trouble*."
>
> He shrugged, reluctant to agree. "It's a way of giving yourself adventures. Of getting out in the world and seeking knowledge." (*Couples*: 359)

By Hook or Crook:
The Poorhouse Fair

WHEN DAVID COPPERFIELD WONDERED WHETHER
or not he would be discovered to be the hero of his own life, the
question had the edgy momentum of a very real curiosity. It sets
David Copperfield slantingly into motion, the way that only the
purest of questions—or first lines—can. A similar curiosity,
never quite articulated and never exactly abandoned, lies just
below the surface of *The Poorhouse Fair*. Is Hook a hero? Is he
the hero of his own life or only, with inadvertent grace, the hero
of others' lives? John Hook is the most elderly and least flexible
of Updike's heroes: the determinate influences of his life are as
deeply engraved as the lines in the palm of his hand. He seems
precarious only in his prolonged evasion of death itself, and
this—the approach of death, and Hook's elusiveness—remains
the most heated courtship in an otherwise chaste and coolly
beautiful book.

In the antique matter-of-factness of his manners, Hook is like
other old men in Updike's fiction, most notably the grandfather
in *The Centaur*, although Hook's lease on the world, his
complex forbearance and doubtful deafness, will come to seem
far and away the least *perplexed* position of any held by an
Updike hero. Updike is no admirer of the unperplexed; he has

written, "Everything is infinitely fine and any opinion is coarser than reality." (*Picked-Up Pieces*: 498) Hook is definitely a bearer, a propounder, of opinion. Argument for him is the proving ground of the soul, proverbs its fortified castle. In a sense he is the antitype, the Old Testament configuration of sternness and conviction by which the cleverness and vacillations of later Updike heroes will be judged, and found wanting.

The Poorhouse Fair is in some ways a very plain work, ambitious mainly in the texture of its melancholy. It is not quite Updike's first novel. Of an earlier work, called *Home*, he remarked that ". . . it really felt like a very heavy bundle of yellow paper, and I realized that this was not going to be my first novel—it had too many of the traits of a first novel. I did not publish it. . . ." (*Picked-Up Pieces*: 477) Quizzical, crafted, and self-assured, *The Poorhouse Fair* seems reassuringly far from the qualities usually attributed to first novels. It has a neat air of biography rather than any haze of autobiographical ingeniousness; it assumes that Hook will hold our attention because any life, and the infractions of death, sorrow, and remorse into that life, are things well worth considering. "My grandfather, who is somewhat like John Hook in that book, was recently dead, and so the idea of some kind of memorial gesture, embodying what seems to have been on my part a very strong sense of national decay, crystallized in this novel." (*ibid.*) What more profound memorial gesture than to let an old man plainly and calmly speak his piece? *The Poorhouse Fair* follows Hook's moods, and the machinations of the other inhabitants of the poorhouse, with near-flawless accuracy, never veering too far from the treacherous realities of an ageing body, and never straying into nervous sentiment. It is an elegant book, resonant with voices. The marvels of the world—which will so often lie, for Updike, in the cache of erotic knowledge peculiar to adultery—are here located quite simply in the particulars of human minds and failings.

"The poorhouse impinged on us in many ways," Updike observed in his memoir "The Dogwood Tree: A Boyhood."

Perhaps in this uneasiness—*impinges* can mean literally "to strike; dash; collide"—lies the germ of the novel:

> For one thing, my father, whose favorite nightmare was poverty, often said that he liked living so close to a poorhouse; if worse came to worse, he could walk there. . . . Twice, in my childhood, the poorhouse barn burnt, and I remember my father (he loved crowds) rushing out of the house in the middle of the night, and my begging to go and my mother keeping me with her, and the luckier, less sheltered children the next day telling me horrific tales of cooked cows and screaming horses. All I saw were the charred ruins, still smoldering, settling here and there with an unexpected crackle, like the underbrush the morning after an ice storm. (*Assorted Prose*: 123)

Sheltered, in the sense that his mother keeps him with her, he is nonetheless exposed to his father's "favorite nightmares," a thing which some parents would probably consider as dangerous as the witnessing of a barn burning down. In this intimately contrived connection, worse does come to worse: Updike has settled, if not his father, then a figure "somewhat like" his grandfather inside the confines of the poorhouse, so that the ruefully recited nightmare comes true, in a way. Updike constructs his own tale in response to the horrific ones of the "luckier, less sheltered" children. For charred ruins he has substituted the ruined lives of elderly men and women, and he is the only spectator to their dwindling hopes, their apprehensiveness, their fidgety dreams and stubborn sorrows.

The Poorhouse Fair is therefore a sad, threadbare, and moving series of vignettes. The conversations of these old people halt in incomprehension, and the silences between them are extended by sleep, deliberation, and absent-mindedness. It is almost a kind of play, in which conversations are revealed to be, at bottom, the paired reveries of mutually disinterested speakers—and still it is a gallant play, for they continue to improvise ethics, craftsmanship, religion, flirtation, comfort, and advice. The vignettes culminate in a fair that the inhabitants of the poorhouse organize each year. The elements of the fair are as reliable as those of a Mass; each ritual holds forth the slender promise of redemption. Because the realm of the poorhouse is a severely impoverished one, real promise gleams almost unbearably bright. The rather plain surfaces of the novel are somewhat relieved by intervals of slapstick—an old man tenderly and awkwardly chasing his wife's green parakeet down an endless flight of stairs beguiling as a maze; a young man, cunningly directed by one of the poorhouse's old men, backing a truck full of soda pop into the wall of the poorhouse, which immediately crumbles.

> "Is it wide enough?" Ted asked the tall man, who looked as though he had some authority.
>
> "Last year they backed it through," a woman said. More old men and women were slowly gathering from everywhere.
>
> "Now don't start to cry," the small man with the dirty-looking face said. "Why the f. does your company hire kids that can't even drive a kiddy-car? Can you only drive forward? Ram it into reverse."
>
> Ted stepped away from him, plucked the tan butt from his mouth, let it drop at his feet, ground it into the gravel, and said effectively, "O.K."
>
> "Slam her through, dump the p., and I'll get into the seat beside you and crouch down. Then step on it. Don't look back. Do you have a gun, kid?" (*The Poorhouse Fair*: 59-60)

In this novel, Updike is minding his p.'s and f.'s, a fact that lends *The Poorhouse Fair* an air of deliberate unworldliness.

The blunt profanity that emerges in *The Centaur,* in its close calls with beggars and bums, is here neatly staved off by abbreviation. Even the assonance—"plucked the tan butt"—serves to distance *The Poorhouse Fair* from the habitual ground of narrative; it resembles the language of a fairy-tale, worn smooth through repetition. Furthermore, this is an almost classic fairy-tale structure, the impotent old man taunting and finally duping a powerful young intruder. In its absurdities, the swiftness of its reversals, and the real merriment of its farce, *The Poorhouse Fair* preserves a fairy-tale innocence whose edges are darkened by the imminence of death, for these old people are souls thinly disguised by the last frail trappings of bodies. When they converse, it could well be the dialogue of pure spirits. There is something resolutely incorrupt, even disembodied, about their language, no matter how coarse or niggling the subjects they pursue. In this narrowly focussed world, perplexity is the most common variable; debate rises to a fine height. In a sense, this is a community free of Eros, and their human judgments seem keener, more precise, trimmed of self-interest.

> Hook had a very clear inner apprehension of what virtue was: An austerity of the hunt, a manliness which comes from all life, so that it can be written that the woman takes her life from the man. As the Indian once served the elusive deer he hunted, men once served an invisible goal, and grew hard in such service and pursuit, and lent their society an indispensable shadow. Impotent to provide this tempering salt, men would sink lower than women, as indeed they had. Women are the heroes of dead lands. (*The Poorhouse Fair*: 160)

Those cadences seem, to me, precisely right, as quirky as thought itself. The woman who took her life from the man, of course, was Eve; Hook seems to believe that things since then have not gone quite as well. His philosophy for the proper relation between a man and a woman seems chiselled from stony elements of experience, Biblical injunction, and solemn sociological imperative, yet it bears a strong resemblance to certain of Updike's own beliefs:

> The basic problem may be simply one of encouragement, because of the failure of nerve, the lassitude and despair, the sense that we've gone to the end of the corridor and found it blank.... In *Couples* Piet is quite a modern man in that he really can't act for himself because he's overwhelmed by the moral implications of any act—leaving his wife, staying with her. While the women in that book are less sensitive perhaps to this oppressive quality, of cosmic blackness, and it is the women who do almost all of the acting. I don't want to say that being passive, being inactive, being paralyzed, is wrong in an era when so much action is crass and murderous. I do feel that in the generations that I've had a glimpse of—I can see my grandfather at one end, and I can see my boys coming up—there has been a perceptible loss of the sense of righteousness . . . I suspect that the vitality of women now, the way that many of us lean on them, is not an eternal phenomenon but a historical one, and fairly recent. (*Picked-Up Pieces*: 484)

Hook's phrase "impotent to provide this tempering salt" foretells Updike's own phrasing, "the failure of nerve, the lassitude and despair . . ." All in all, it is a curious conviction. Who would want to believe that the vitality of women is a "fairly recent" phenomenon, and that men must be deprived of something—a sense of righteousness or an invisible goal—before they can rely on women? The austerely dominant creed—"Women are the heroes of dead lands"—in fact returns again, broken into separate instances in which women are treated as heroes-by-default and America as either a dead, or visibly dying, land. Updike seems to believe in an America composed of something lost and Atlantis-like, as well as of the last threatened corners of Eden. Piet Hanema reflects on "this rape of a haven precious to ornamental shy creatures who need no house. Builders burying the world God made." (*Couples*: 90) The short story "Atlantises" is an extended metaphor, alternately playful and grim, in which Updike's beloved East Coast terrain is equated with an Atlantis now "sunk beneath the sea. It had been sandy, marshy, permeated by glistening water like something very rotten, and doomed." (*Problems*: 254) This is a far cry from the infatuated pastorales once sung to Tarbox's "margin of tawny salt marshes," shining and windswept. Richness has now turned to rot; the hero of "Atlantises" knows that he "got out just in time."

This interpretation—"something very rotten, and doomed"— echoes the "very strong sense of national decay" that Updike felt when he began *The Poorhouse Fair*. The feeling seems to have endured, essentially intact, from before 1958, when *The Poorhouse Fair* was published, until at least 1969, the date of the interview from which I've quoted. At times, this belief in the diminishment of America seems forbearing and gentle; at others it is queerly married to a soaringly optimistic appraisal of American values and environs, an almost obtrusive and rather prickly intention to "sing America." *Rabbit, Run* and *Rabbit Is Rich* are documents of this inconsistency, and more ambivalent and deft for the tension it generates.

But Hook's analysis, even with its leavening pinch of whimsy in the image of "the elusive deer," relfects more harshly on the motives of many of Updike's younger, later heroes, who occasionally seem embodiments of the very failure Hook predicted. Measured against this standard, Updike's other heroes will seem to practice a sorry mix of resistance, stasis, immobility, and evasion. Even in a world where acts can have murderous results, paralysis is not a viable alternative for long. The traditional injunction—"the woman takes her life from the man"—continues to exist, but only in queerly distorted remnants of a once imperious whole. These later heroes wish to avoid burdensome responsibility, while still secretly assuming its prerogatives:

> Tod liked her ageing, felt warmed by it, for it . . . was involuntary. It had happened to her with him, yet it was not his fault. He wanted nothing to be his fault. This made her load double. ("Love Song, for a Moog Synthesizer," in *Problems*: 177)

In a sense, any woman who acquiesces to this pact—nothing is his fault—is permitting the hero to walk the streets wearing the Emperor's new clothes. Updike's fiction often turns on the careful analysis of fault. These are men beguiled by guilt, transparently assuming their own innocence in complicated situations. In this instance, one imagines, it is the woman who will "grow hard in service and pursuit," and she who will reap the spiritual returns. The man, if not exactly impotent, is at least wistfully remote from consequence. In Hook's view, and possibly in Updike's own, the nurturing, protective stance ought to belong to the man. The elementary tenets of husbandry would require him to shoulder his share of the burden, to be coupled with the woman in the face of all mysteries, even the guileful one of ageing.

There is a Grimm's fairy tale, called "The Story of One Who Set Out to Study Fear," that chronicles the efforts of its hero, who, for magical reasons, cannot feel fear, to experience terror strong enough to make his skin creep. The germ of the tale lies in this prolonged seeking of an evasive but ordinary thing. In the story there is a line, that defines the problem: "What would become a hook must crook itself betimes." Hook, the hero of *The Poorhouse Fair*, is likewise in the position of seeker, and within the constricted atmosphere of the poorhouse—as within the novel—he slowly, by stiff small degrees, learns to "crook."

Hook is a teacher, and teachers, in Updike's fiction, are very fallible men. Hook likes to keep a certain distance between himself and the world. His closest relationship, his most precisely elegaic understanding, is reserved for the land itself.

> "Now I can remember, as a boy, how you could go to the top of a hill and not see a house in an-y direction. Now"— he coughed again, since the heads of neither had moved— "there can't be a foot of earth east of the Alleghenies where a body can stand and not be within hailing distance of a house. We have made the land very tame.". . .
>
> Turning away, he felt like a rise of unplowed land which approached from below swells unexpectedly and in a spattering of daisies makes a join with the sky. (*The Poorhouse Fair*: 25)

Beautiful, this: to read "within hailing distance of a house," with its somehow mild and old-fashioned *h*'s, forces on the reader a subtle mimicry of breath expelled in the act of hailing. The quaint phrasing—"where a body can stand"—serves also to articulate Hook's exact position: he *is* still a body, literal and frail, located between heaven and earth, past and present. Nostalgia has rendered his identification with the land almost absolute. In the simile of unplowed land, complete down to the spattering of flowers, there is a premonition of the unmown field so central to *Of the Farm*, and the primary metaphor, in which a human being is equated with land, will be reflected in Joey Robinson's enumeration of the ways in which his wife is a field, lovely and wide. Like the land, Hook is supposed to rise upward, and even to join with the sky; this join will contain something of the unexpected, no matter how long or exquisitely Hook considers death.

Hook breaks words into syllables with a haltingness that comes to seem a form of errant reverence, letting each syllable take its proper weight, no more and no less: "You don't antici-pate, then, any difficulties, on the other side?" (*The Poorhouse Fair*: 30) This modest employment of hyphens, and the para-bolic, carefully freighted speech in which it figures, also characterizes the speech of Peter's grandfather in *The Centaur*:

> My grandfather stirred in the other room and announced, "Now that was a favorite saying of Jake Beam's, who used to be stationmaster at the old Bertha Furnace station, before they discon-tinued the passenger station. 'Time and tide,' he would say, so solemn, 'and the Alton Railroad wait for no man.' " (*The Centaur*: 52)

And although his beliefs seem stern and formally unyielding, Hook actually proves himself to be rather bemused in the presence of women.

> Hook did not think it was a woman's obligation to tell him he had had his time. Amy Mortis was a woman of his own generation—she would have been marriageable to him—and along with the corresponding virtues she had the talkativeness, the presuming habit, the *familiarity* of such women; calling him "John." He enjoyed conversing with them, but not as much as they with him, nor for as long. Yet as with his late wife, he was too weak, too needful of her audience to break away, and instead lingered to lecture. (*The Poorhouse Fair*: 29)

Even in this elderly analysis, there is the distant scent of a woman's marriageability, a hero's ambivalence. It seems that Hook, as the husband of a dead wife, is still inalterably a husband, and the flaws of the marriage—his supposed weakness and needfulness—endure even after death. It is an austere philosophy, imperfectly practiced, for Hook by rights should have been the stronger partner in the alliance. In the fashion of

Updike's later heroes, he can only survey the course of his marriage, and therefore of his life, with the severe earnestness of self-reproach. In this last, harsh, perservering scrutiny, in the stubborn absence of any tenderer inflection, and in the force of his reluctance to leave life, Hook proves himself a hero.

Women and Fields:
Of the Farm

CERTAIN IMAGES PREVAIL THROUGHOUT A WRI-
ter's life, gaining in elegance, resourcefulness, and strength as the
writer continues to refine them through the fractional readjust-
ments, the minor shiftings and alignings, of prolonged attention.
These images serve as auguries of future preoccupations as well
as reflections of past ones. In a sense they are the detritus, the
chips and splinters of attention, pushed forward like stones
nudged by a glacier. In the shape of the moraine some vanished
intention remains clearly visible.

For Updike, one such central image is the metaphor, often
scrupulously devised and formal, but other times curiously
offhand, equating a woman with terrain. The airiness with which
he sometimes treats the image is interesting; it implies a
metaphor so strikingly close to the grain of the author's
perceptions that it can be trusted, however glancingly or briefly,
to advance the narrative, to quicken its surface. From this
primary equation—Woman = Terrain—variations are struck
with workmanlike precision to correspond to a variety of
fictional situations:

▌ Still, what a relief to have *intelligere* become *esse*. Land ho!

> She appeared to me during those afternoons of copulation as a promontory on some hitherto sunken continent of light. (*A Month of Sundays*: 39)

> She was good in bed. She went to church. Her I.Q. was 145. She repeated herself. Nothing fit; it frightened him. Yet Tod wanted to hang on, to hang on to the bits and pieces, which perhaps were not truly pieces but islands, which a little lowering of sea level would reveal to be rises on a sunken continent, peaks of subaqueous range, secretly one, a world. ("Love Song, for a Moog Synthesizer," in *Problems*: 174)

> One afternoon, unforseen, he felt her beside him and she was of a piece, his. They were standing somewhere, in a run-down section of the city, themselves tired, looking at nothing, and her presence beside him was like the earth's beneath his feet, continuous, extensive, and dry, there by its own rights, unthinkingly assumed to be there. She had become his wife. (*ibid*: 180)

Differently inflected, the image still carries a recognizable tone—this, it implies, is the natural order of things. A woman, rightfully possessed, smacks of *terra firma*. Even in the more equivocal examples, where there is something mythic or Atlantis-like about her, investigation will prove that she is whole, "secretly one, a world." Enchanted continents can be exposed, exotic landscapes tamed. Such wealth seems slightly dizzying; each woman is a realm, her body a kaleidoscope which can yield any number of shifting configurations.

Of the Farm is a sort of book-length metaphor, subtly hinged, in which a wife is demonstrated to be terrain, or, more exactly, a series of terrains, glimpsed as though from the window of a train:

> My wife is wide, wide-hipped and long-waisted, and,

26

surveyed from above, gives an impression of terrain, of a wealth whose ownership imposes upon my own body a sweet strain of extension; entered, she yields a variety of landscapes, seeming now a snowy rolling perspective of bursting cotton bolls seen through the negro arabesques of a fancywork wrought-iron balcony; now a taut vista of mesas dreaming in the midst of sere and painterly ochre; now a gray French castle complexly fitted to a steep green hill whose terraces imitate turrets; now something like Antarctica; and then a receding valleyland of blacks and purples where an unrippled river flows unseen between shadowy banks of grapes that are never eaten. (*Of the Farm*: 39)

Every conceivable sort of land, wild or domestic, fertile or barren, is summoned through this starry list. It is the ultimate explication of the image, promising in its pentimento of adjectives and semicolons that no shading of awareness has been excluded. Yet the real root of the metaphor seems to lie eerily elsewhere, at the shadowy edges of this bemused catalogue, in a kind of Platonic essence of land. Updike once admired "the kind of timid reverence toward what exists that Cézanne shows when he grapples for the shape and shade of a fruit through a mist of delicate stabs." (*Picked-Up Pieces*: 34) In this case, *what exists* is a wife, and her shade and shape still seem, in spite of the exhaustiveness of the list and its obvious reverence, to have eluded her husband's analysis.

Even the title of this novel is modest, pinned down by its preposition as a farm's locale is fixed by a boundary stone. There is some evidence that Updike has deliberately pared and shaped the work to give this impression of sternness and slightness—the book is brief and shapely; tensions neatly fill the spans of silence; the entire ambience is so plain and self-sufficient that a broken dish is a catastrophe powerful as an earthquake. In his

27

introduction to the Czech edition *Of the Farm*, Updike characterized the book as "chamber music, containing only four voices—the various ghosts in it do not speak, and the minister's sermon, you will notice, is delivered in close paraphrase, without the benefit of quotation marks. The voices, like musical instruments, echo each other's phrases and themes, then take turns dominating, embark on brief narrative solos, and recombine in argument or harmony." (*Picked-Up Pieces*: 92) The landscape of the farm is as rich and painterly as any of Updike's. The unmown field—with its suggestion of neglected duty and tardy filial obedience—occupies the geometric center of the novel. The mowing of this field comes to seem a gesture of great significance, alternately suggesting military movements or the act of making love, the ragged grass falling in a premonition of mortality, even the clouds weighted with complexity.

> The clouds surrounding her divorce became the clouds I moved beneath, mowing. The sky that had seemed a nation of citadels and an arena of political maneuver verged on divulging the anatomy of a dead marriage: a luminous forearm seemed laid in sleep across a distorted breast; somber confluences of nimbus suggested lawyers at loggerheads; the edge of Peggy's voice told too sharply against a pentagonal patch of blue. (*Of the Farm*: 63)

It is an environment heady with omens. The central act is sex as divination, an attempt to fix the shadowy nature of the wife into persona. As land, she can be conquered as inevitably as the field is mowed:

> The sun grew higher. The metal hood acquired a nimbus of heat waves that visually warped each stalk. The tractor body was flecked with foam and I, rocked back and forth on the iron seat shaped like a woman's hips, alone in nature, as hidden under the glaring sky as at midnight,

> discovered in myself a swelling which I idly permitted to
> stand, thinking of Peggy. My wife is a field. (*Of the Farm*:
> 47-48)

The hero's mother, in a determined solitude riddled with
reproaches directed toward her son and his new wife, is Ceres-
like, in muted reverberation of the Ceres-mother in *The Centaur*,
although in *Of the Farm* she seems more austere and harsh than
welcoming and fruitful. She and her son move toward each other
in the covert gestures of embattled intimacy, deflecting each
irony before it can be fully felt, guessing at each other's motives,
sparring and reconciling.

> "The boy," my mother said, "seems bright."
> "Yes, I think he is."
> "It's interesting," she continued, "because the mother
> doesn't seem so."
> The blow was delivered in the darkness like a pillow of
> warmth against my face. I felt myself at the point at which,
> years ago, in this same room, I had failed Joan. Yet I
> respected—was captive within—my mother's sense of
> truth. My response was weak. "Not?"

When Joey acquiesces in his mother's appraisal—when he, in
effect, admits that his wife is a stupid woman—it has the force of
revelation. He has succeeded in fencing her in, and, in his own
eyes, effectively circumscribed his demesne, his wife as terrain,
with this stony acknowledgment. Oddly, the admission does not
seem to greatly pain him; perhaps stupidity is the obvious flaw in
a creature whose "beauty will ever have in men's eyes a dreamlike
quality." The problem with dreamlike qualities is that they don't
reconcile easily with the agile willfulness of intelligence. Whether
or not Peggy is really stupid seems problematic; in *Rabbit, Run* a
wife's "dumbness" is shown to be a very dangerous thing, but
Peggy seems rather quick on her feet for a stupid woman, and

engages a tricky opponent, Joey's mother, in arduous conversation with a defiant prowess. While she is not particularly subtle, Peggy seems self-possessed and even adamant. Her very name, Peg, suggests roundness, strength, and utility, as in a tent peg; earlier in the novel Joey's mother's hair has been a "tent" for him, when he was a child. In the short story "Love Song, for a Moog Synthesizer," love itself will be compared to "a striped tent pegged in sand." Perhaps *peg* also has a shading of rib-like exactitude, the resonance of Biblical simplicity, for a peg resembles that bone from which woman was first fashioned.

Of the Farm turns, in fact, on various sermons. The central sermon, carrying a filigreed literary weight even in paraphrase, was originally a piece Updike submitted to *The New Yorker*; it was rejected on the grounds that it was "young." Joey's mother seconds this observation:

> Behind me in the line, my mother in turn told him [the minister], in the level low tone with which she expresses reservations, "It's so unusual to hear a *young* sermon." (*Of the Farm*: 113)

While Joey himself is more generous to the sermon's author:

> At the door, taking the minister's limp and chill little hand, I told him, avoiding his black bold eyes—very local eyes— that his sermon had been excellent. (*ibid.*)

In a sense, this is the writer avoiding his own eyes, the limp handshake planted in the narrative like a secret consolation, a shy and writerly joke. Updike's eye, in *Of the Farm*, is after all a "very local" eye.

The other sermons within the book are those the characters make, restlessly, to each other, closing and fanning out and regrouping in the skittish structure of their chamber music. Each sermon shadows the central one; the central question might be,

"What is the proper ground of relationships between men and women?" The proper ground cannot be, apparently, sex, which too quickly slides into whorishness. Each time Joey leaves Peggy alone he dwells on the risk of rape, as if she must inevitably draw to herself the sexual attention of the world, like a flower drawing bees. Her son remarks that, "The odd fact is, a bee did almost sting her," while she is wearing a bikini. "I told her to stand very still and, sure enough, eventually it flew away." Her only refuge is to retreat into immobility when threatened. Later she is picking blackberries, again in her bikini, and again she is endangered. "I did a very stupid thing," she tells Joey. "A car went by a while ago with a lot of sinister men and I hid in what I think must be poison ivy." (*Of the Farm*: 118)

The threat of rape to Peggy parallels the threatened selling of the farm itself. The farm, too, is a valuable piece of property, the last of its size in the region—I think of Hook's regretful assumption that "we have made the land very tame." In an attempt to apprise her son of the farm's value, Joey's mother concludes by urging him not to sell cheap. It seems unlikely that he will. As an Updike hero, these things—wife, fields, precarious relationship with his mother—are going to cost him very dear.

The "Me" in "Marry Me"

DECIPHERING A BOOK FROM THE STARTING POINT
of its epigraph is a tactic as inevitably disappointing, in its way,
as working Rubik's cube from an instruction manual. Obedi-
ently, though—and because that is the only way I could ever
work Rubik's cube—I will quote the jingling quatrain with
which Updike prefaces the novel *Marry Me*:

> Choose me your valentine,
>   Next, let us marry—
> Love to the death will pine
>   If we long tarry.
>
> —Robert Herrick

Updike, in his guise of light versifier, must love these bladed
rhymes. *Marry Me* is a book in which various things—including
the lives of the four people who are its primary subjects—rhyme
against each other: ". . . it seems to me that rhyme is one of the
ways we make things hard for ourselves, make a game out of
nothing, so we can win or lose and lighten the, what?, the
indeterminacy of life." Or so said the novelist Henry Bech,
straining to answer a schoolgirl's question. In *Marry Me*,

marriage itself will prove to be the game fashioned out of nothing; it sometimes seems to be the only game in town. "But I don't *want* you as a mistress," the hero of *Marry Me*, Jerry Conant, tells his lover, Sally Mathias. "Mistresses are for European novels. Here, there's no institution except marriage. Marriage and the Friday night baskeball game."(*Marry Me*: 55)

So that leaves, for the troubled realm of American novels, only married men and magic tricks. Because what is the proposal of a married man to his married lover—the question, *marry me?*, in each of its variously plausible intonations—but sleight of hand, the dove pulled fluttering from the hero's empty sleeve?

> [Jerry] said to Sally carefully, "haven't you been listening?. . . I'm asking you to marry me." (*Marry Me*: 211)

> "Secondly, I will divorce Sally if you agree to marry her." [Sally's husband said]
> "If? I thought I had agreed." Jerry's voice scratched, to hold fast against the sliding sensation that came with these words. (*Marry Me*: 235)

> "Perhaps I misunderstood you last night," Sally persisted. "I thought I heard you say you wanted to marry me." (*Marry Me*: 247)

This novel runs on just such legerdemain. The question, whenever it appears, seems queerly clouded, as if no one can quite bear its repetition, its translation into the real world of consequence; it has a sort of *now you hear it, now you don't* quality. It is romantic coda rather than legal fiat; it is Jerry's obligation as hero to mediate in stumbling, tentative fashion between these things—to bridge this distance, if he can. "The world is composed of what we think it is; what we expect tends to happen; and what we expect is really what we desire." (*Marry Me*: 178) But is the world, in fact, composed of what we think it is? Desire camouflaged as expectation is the principle of magic; the confusion of expectation with inevitability is the province of childhood. Some combination of the two allows lovers to exist. But the alliance, as Updike implies throughout *Marry Me*, is a fragile one, a sort of endangered habitat of the mind. "I'm afraid I'm not very strong with you; I guess I should pretend I don't think it would be wonderful," Jerry tells Sally. "But it *would* be wonderful, if I could swallow the guilt. We'd spend the first month making love and looking at things. We'd be very tired when we got there, and we'd have to start looking at the world all over again, and rebuild it from the bottom up, beginning with the pebbles." (*Marry Me*: 54)

In this novel imaginary marriages can be conceived and discarded, all the while retaining something of their original enchanted lightness, the terrain the lovers have fashioned from thin air. There is a curiously persistent chord of evasiveness, however: things are being tried out; this is not quite the real world; escapes are partial, and no disaster irremediable. Even the ending of the novel is sketched in lightly, three separate times, as Botticelli would sketch an angel's arm until the angle conformed with some ideal tenderness. Hypothetical divorces are conjured up almost as playfully—"Tell me about you," Jerry says to Ruth, his wife. "How do you feel? Happy? Sad? Want a divorce?"—only to darken, and grow grimmer, refusing to vanish. The request—"Tell me about you"—implies that the husband and wife are strangers. The question—"Want a divorce?"—implies that he wishes they could be.

"What we have is love," Jerry instructs Sally, while they are caught in an airport waiting for the flight which will return them safely home—he to his home, she to hers. "But love must become fruitful, or it loses itself. I don't mean having babies—God, we've all had too many of those—I mean just being relaxed, and right, and, you know, with a blessing. Does 'blessing' seem silly to you?" (*Marry Me*: 55-56) This is the adjuration of Genesis adapted for the perplexities of 1961. It is a year and an ambience in which the word "blessing" could sound silly, although for Updike—in whose work blessing is a serious act, and not sought-after lightly—this is more a veiled indictment of the times than of his hero. The puzzled tone, and even the protectively self-deprecating lilt of the query, are nonetheless characteristic of Jerry. Uncertainty is his touchstone; he is beguiled by women to the degree that they present the *possibility* of certainty. In part because he is its hero, *Marry Me* remains a series of interrogatory monologues, sometimes compulsively overlapping, stricken, and public, and other times as sad and circular as daydreams. The title, bare of a question mark, is imperative by default, but the voices locked within the novel itself will be curious, quarrelsome, pleading, perplexed.

> "What's to bear?" [Jerry] asked.
>
> "Giving up Sally," [Ruth] said.
>
> "Is that part of the promise?"
>
> "You must try with me," Ruth told him, "to the end of summer. Otherwise, what's the use?"
>
> "The use of what?"
>
> "Of trying."
>
> "And then what?"
>
> "Then decide."
>
> "God," Jerry said, releasing her. "You've been such a lovely wife." (*Marry Me*: 121)

Marry Me is finally a novel about tarrying, not only in the keenly sexual sense of dalliance that glints through the lines of the Herrick quatrain, but in the sense of contrived separation peculiar to the myth of Tristan and Iseult. These lovers are held apart through the force of circumstance, and if circumstance, in fact, dovetails rather neatly with their own most covert apprehensions about each other, that is only the last trace of a pragmatism which cannot be eradicated from even the glossiest, best-tended romance. Because they are so extraordinarily inventive as lovers, even their doubts have an exquisite resonance, and are elevated almost to the rank of passions. In a sense the task of Tristan and Iseult is to invent a separation which can match—in kenetic potential and erotic complicity—the power of the original attraction. They create between them a charmed void. Voids allow for certain emotions—yearning, wistfulness, wonder, or sorrow—which the actual presence of the beloved negates or blurs. At first they fashioned for each other an enchanted terrain, a world whose every pebble was magicked from nothing, and then they proceed to fashion an equally enchanted *nothing*. This nothing is composed of doubt, delay, and hesitation before the awesome act of divorce; that such hesitation will engender a small death—that of their love—is the slender, slanting axis on which this novel turns. "I don't understand what quite happened," Jerry tells Ruth, near the novel's end. "As an actual wife or whatever, [Sally] stopped being an *idea* , and for the first time, I *saw* her." (*Marry Me*: 268) Ideas, it seems, are more easily loved than women, imaginary wives more willingly courted than actual ones. In his review of Denis de Rougemont's *Love Declared* Updike notes:

> On the most meagre diet of echoes and glimpses [Tristan] nourishes his passion. In the image of Iseult he has supplied himself with a focus for the efforts of his sublimated energy. In addition, he has obtained honorable exemption from the distracting claims of accessible women. Clinchingly, Don Juans are born and not made, whereas any man can elect to be a Tristan. (*Assorted Prose*: 232)

It is a proposed ecology of the heart, if Tristanism can be imagined as a sort of ecological niche that any sufficiently supple male can occupy. The truth is that Jerry Conant does very well on "echoes and glimpses," like a laboratory rat growing only more clever at running mazes as its diet is reduced. It does seem to imply that the efforts of the hero's "sublimated energy" are not extremely rich to begin with, since they must be hoarded, focussed, eked out by "honorable exemption." "While nostalgia does not create women," Updike writes, "perhaps it does create Iseults." (*Assorted Prose*: 223) In Sally, Jerry has to reckon with an Iseult in a lemonade-yellow bathing suit, one who has three children and a sometimes violent temper, as well as expensive tastes and a boorish husband. If he has created his Iseult through nostalgia, it must be nostalgia for a very uncertain future.

Still, however slanted its axis, this novel resolutely, reassuringly turns; it is as neat as a quatrain. Even its structure contrives to rhyme, for these married couples—Jerry and Ruth Conant; Richard and Sally Mathias—have alternated liaisons. Such alternation predicts something of the far more bluntly practiced inter-couple swapping of *Couples*, but the first is a *pas de deux*, the second a free-for-all. Still, there are dangers inherent in a *pas de deux*—one misstep can ruin the dance, and the timing must be flawless—which have no parallel in the brawling heat of a free-for-all. In this way, *Marry Me* is the more fragile book. The original affair occurs between Richard and Ruth, who all along seem rather quaintly matter-of-fact with each other: "[Richard] had brought her a book they had discussed, the new Murdoch, as an excuse. As an excuse, it was cursorily offered; his instinct told him he would not need much of one." (*Marry Me*: 86) Love beginning from a proffered book is as old and honorable as Heloise and Abelard; one guesses—from a review of an Iris Murdoch novel included in *Picked-Up Pieces*, and entitled "Amore Vincit Omnia Ad Nauseam," that Updike considers the affair, as the novel, somewhat deficient in inspiration. The pairing of the phrase "as an excuse," like the two identical sides of a trick-shop coin, demonstrates the flaw in this affair: there are no great obstacles to overcome, and therefore, in a correlative of Tristan's Law (". . . appealingness is inversely proportional to attainability. Attainability is somewhat proportional to psychic distance." [*Problems*: 152]), it cannot be a great passion. The alarm sparked by this affair soon diminishes, for Richard and Ruth manage the thing so few lovers in Updike's work can manage, keeping a secret. Ruth comes to view the affair as a practical measure, a solid, wifely gesture, like the taking of One-A-Day Plus Iron. There are certain trace elements—quirks of sex, the rarer shadings of masochism—which she could have been missing in the calm diet of domesticity.

> On the whole she was well satisfied with her affair, and as she zipped up the children's snowsuits, or closed a roast into the oven, thought of this adventure snug in her past with some complacence. She judged herself improved and deepened in about the normal amount—she had dared danger and carried wisdom away, a more complete and tolerant woman. She had had boyfriends, a husband, a lover; it seemed she could rest. (*Marry Me*: 94-95)

Ruth is a heroine to the degree that she did brave danger. She and Richard did not get caught; the adventure seals itself the way a fairy tale is sealed by the formula "and they lived happily ever after," but the ritual question so central to the novel—*marry me*?—is never even posed during the course of the affair. It arises only later, during a confrontation between the two couples caused by the revelation of the affair between Jerry and Sally, when Richard finds himself, however awkwardly, assuming the stance of hero:

> "Ruth," he said, "you're right. You're always right. I wish you were my friend."
>
> "I am your friend," she said.
>
> "Would you like to marry me?"
>
> Ruth, blushing, refused the proposal as gently as if it had been seriously made. (*Marry Me*: 202)

But it is that surface calm which follows her affair which reveals the hint of the fracturing still to come, for this heroine seems about to live, not happily, but somewhat maniacally ever after.

> That year, the first of Kennedy's presidency, the rivers and ponds froze early and black-smooth for beautiful skating. Skating, Ruth flew, and, flying, she was free. She drove cars too fast, and drank too much, and skated upriver away from Jerry and the children—darting, swooping strides, between hushed walls of thin silver trees. This will to fly had come upon her since her failure with Richard— for it was a failure, any romance that does not end in marriage fails. (*Marry Me*: 96)

So the first affair in *Marry Me* has been dealt out like the line that opens the quatrain—the line that, as Bech quotes Valéry, "comes as a gift from the gods and costs nothing." Whether or not it has come as a gift from the gods, this affair has not cost any of them anything, except for the price of certain langorous lunches in a darkened Chinese restaurant. The scheme will inevitably change, and grow costly: Jerry and Sally have fallen in love. Around this love, which is immediately problematic and guilty, even landscape shifts into the one consummately troubled habitat, Eden. At the beach where Sally and Jerry go to make love, ". . . the dunes still wore the look, inherited from winter, of clean-swept Nature, never tasted."(*Marry Me*: 11) Nature with a capital N has been summoned; can Adam and Eve be far behind?

> Yes yes, the touch, the touch of their skins the length of their bodies in the air, under the sun. The sun made [Jerry's] closed eyes swim in red; her side and upward shoulder warmed and her mouth gradually melted. They felt no hurry; this was perhaps the gravest proof that they were, Jerry and Sally, the original man and woman—that they felt no hurry, that they did not so much excite each

other as put the man and woman in each other to rest. (*Marry Me*: 13)

This Molly Bloom-like "Yes yes," which sounds faintly phlegmatic out of context, and the quality of rest—later echoed in "being relaxed, and right"—will later elude them. In a way the answer—yes—has preceded the question: there is not yet a plot. The world was plotless before the Fall. Lovers who are happy with each other seem almost static: their sex, as Jerry describes it, has a simplicity which seems more appropriate to Edenic flora than to real and complex human beings. "The stem bends. A single drop of dew falls to the ground. *Blip*." (*Marry Me*: 148) But these are lovers whose every approach actually requires the upward inflection, the negotiated tenderness of a question. The first words spoken in the novel are Sally's, as she greets Jerry from the dunes: "When she called to him the sound came fluted by the cool air like a birdcall. 'Jerry?' It was a question, though if she could see him she must know it was he." (*Marry Me*: 11)

It is hard to say which would have been more valued in Eden, innocence or amazement. Sally, as a lover, can afford to demonstrate both. She has a "heart-shaped" face; she is "blond and freckled and clean-swept, a shy creature of the sand that had hidden her." The Aphrodite myth, which Updike uses to such lovely ends in *The Centaur*, is mixed in here, for Sally "had been married ten years, and furthermore had had lovers before Jerry," yet her lovemaking is "wonderfully virginal, simple, and quick." One wonders whether sex, in any Updike novel, can long remain either simple or quick, and indeed Sally is in distinct contrast to Ruth, whose persona in bed Jerry describes as "a roll in the mud. Mother Mud." Corruption and invention go hand and hand into exile. The way back is guarded, not by an angel, but by the accumulated silt of domestic sorrows.

Marry Me, although it focusses on these domestic sorrows, encapsulates certain shadowy tensions of 1962; as such it precedes the graver documentation of *Couples*, which is a virtual paradigm of 1963. The vague apprehensions and uneasy nights of Jerry Conant will evolve into the mortal fears and morally choreographed nightmares of Piet Hanema in *Couples*. One has a Tom Sawyerish bad conscience, the other Kierkegaardian fear and trembling. In two years, the world seems to have become a far more dangerous place. The Greenwood of *Marry Me* is transformed into the Tarbox of *Couples*, though Greenwood will retain some grassy scent of Eden, and Tarbox a smoky stink of Sodom. *Marry Me* is a romance, and like all romances, rather eerily free of datum points. Although Sally, in front of the White House, "thought of the wall-eyed young Irishman who reigned there, wondered if he were good in bed, and didn't see how he could be, he was President"(*Marry Me*: 31), this Kennedy is only a premonition of the tragic young King-figure who will haunt the couples of *Couples*. In *Marry Me* there is amused speculation; in *Couples*, there is an assassination. The world figures for the lovers in *Marry Me* almost as a set of paintings to be studied, vignettes to be observed, moments to be attributed to the appropriate painter, as if in a slide-show flickering through the darkened auditorium of an Introduction to Art History class.

> Sally's face, tinted by the glare as violently as a Bonnard—her lips purple, her hair ashen—seemed a pale, feral apparition striking into the cloudless blue . . . (*Marry Me*: 165)

> His face was inches above hers, swollen and dark, a Goya. (*Marry Me*: 144)

> The polished night about her spun like the atmosphere of a Chagall . . . (*Marry Me*: 121)

> The so-intensely green trees beside the road—she had seen them before, in a Monet, or was it a Pissaro? The bits of

> salmon pink along the birch trunks were Cézanne's.
> (*Marry Me*: 153)

> [Jerry] had found what he wanted—the wall bearing three
> Vermeers. "Oh, God," he moaned, "the drawing; people
> never realize how much *drawing* there is in a Vermeer. The
> wetness of this woman's lips. These marvellous hats. And
> this one, the light on her hands and the gold and the pearls.
> That *touch*, you know; it's a double touch—the exact
> color, in the exact place." He looked at Sally and smiled.
> "Now you and me," he said "are the exact color, but we
> seem to be in the wrong place." (*Marry Me*: 41)

Trysts in museums fascinate Updike. The short story "Museums and Women" is a study in the environments of wonder,
environments devised so that wonder can more easily inhabit
them, whether it be a museum ". . . shaped like a truncated top
and its floor . . . a continuous spiral around an overweening core
of empty vertical space," (*Museums and Women*: 12) or simply
the body of a woman, which Updike seems to believe is
constructed around a like nothingness, an empty vertical space.
". . . his hands of themselves slide up silver and confirm what his
face has found through the cloth of her skirt, a fact monstrous
and lovely: where her legs meet there is nothing. Nothing but silk
and a faint dampness and a curve. This then is the secret the
world holds at its center, this innocence, this absence. . . ." (*The
Centaur*: 184) The narrator of "Museums and Women" tours
this spiral museum with a woman who could possibly become a
lover, but equally possibly never see him again, so that
possibility itself is a helix.

Jerry and Sally, however, have already begun to exhaust
possibility. It is as if, for a moment, they have actually entered a
Vermeer, a sort of fragile stasis, a beautifully becalmed realm in
which the light streams reassuringly from a single direction; in
any case it is this studious, rhapsodic observation of the author

43

which preserves these lovers in a moment of grace. The moment is almost inevitably precarious; there is a quality of precarious, grave *lack* in Jerry himself which makes him a curiously bereft sort of Adam:

> Turning from her bureau, Ruth saw Jerry standing before his closet in his underwear, one hand on his hip and the other scratching his head as he too pondered what to put on for this undefined occasion. She saw him, in this rare moment, as beautiful, a statue out of reach, not a furiously beautiful Renaissance David but a medieval Adam, naked on a tympanum, his head bent to fit the triangular space, the bones of his body expressing innocence and alarm. Awkward and transparent—a Christian body, she supposed. (*Marry Me*: 112)

No one ever realizes how much *drawing* there is in an Updike. This is a rather shy and pallid Adam in comparison to Piet's coarser, ruddier, and altogether more Don Juan-like figure; one is flesh and bones, the other muddied form and muddled spirit, but they each venture out of the garden and into the queer continent of adultery with dutiful trepidation. Jerry's quest has more the quality of something self-imposed, this self-made and narcissistically prolonged Tristanism, while Piet's quest seems somehow inviolate, helplessly endured, oddly pure—something that he was born to. That Jerry should, in each shading of his uncertainty, remain such a haunting figure of "innocence and alarm" is one of the finer aspects of *Marry Me*. In the end it is not a novel which supposes there are any easy answers to its eager, fretful, ardent questions: it simply assumes that such are the questions men and women urgently desire to ask.

Uncoupling Couples

WITH AN UNEASY AND EVEN RUEFUL PERSISTENCE, the novel *Couples* charts various incidents of uncoupling, an act for which the *Random House Dictionary of the English Language* proffers the definition: "to release the coupling or link between; disconnect, as two things connected by a coupling; let go, as a connecting link: *to uncouple railroad cars.*" In this novel, the two things so precariously connected by a coupling are most often a man and a woman; they part in more brutal—and less predictable—ways than boxcars.

Curious, this definition, because of the willfulness implicit in "release." Uncoupling must be, after all, a voluntary act, if an enormously complicated and sad one. *Couples* can be interpreted as a cautionary tale about the awkward art of letting go. Its hero, Piet Hanema, is a man who confronts loss haltingly, a sort of knight of erotic errantry. His grail will be temporarily manifest in each of several women; he is a resolutely enchanted man finding his way through a forest of disenchantments. Updike, in the essaylike paragraph on female sexuality which he includes in the foreword to *Picked-Up Pieces*, might almost be advising Piet directly. "Love, then, becomes an exploration toward a muffled center, a quest whose terrain is the woman and the grail her deep self. The man who advances this exploration bestows a totality meagrely paid for with anything less than enslavement. The man who does not fails disastrously." While it is difficult to determine from this passage whether or not the woman is actively involved in the pursuit of the grail, or whether, being "muffled"—the word suggests a curiously suburban and American purdah—and apparently possessing various shallow selves to keep track of in addition to the crucial "deep" self, she simply has her hands full, and can only follow the hero's progress as a sort of psychological cheerleader, two things do emerge as certainties: the woman *is* the proper terrain for conducting this search, and there exists for the hero, once embarked on the quest, the possibility of disastrous failure.

Couples is set in Tarbox. The town has cropped up before, most strikingly in the short story "The Indian," which is written in a second person singular whose effect is to render the reader an involuntary poltergeist: "The marshes turn green and withdraw through gold into brown, and their indolent, untouched, enduring existence penetrates your fibre. You find you must drive down toward the beach once a week or it is like a week without love." (*The Music School*: 16) Piet Hanema's wife, Angela, covets a house which he refuses her out of considerations both aesthetic and pragmatic: "[Angela] had mourned when the new couple in town, the Whitmans, had bought . . . the old Robinson place, a jerrybuilt summer house in need of total repair. It had a huge view of the salt marshes and a wind exposure that would defy all insulation." (*Couples*: 10) In this novel, houses often provide the essential metaphor for the marriages they shelter, and so the Whitman's marriage will come to seem jerrybuilt, "in need of total repair," when exposed to Tarbox winds. The year is 1963: disconnectedness and loss are plainly in the air. Within the month of June, "Pope John had died, Quang Duc had immolated himself, Valentina Tereshkova had become the first woman in space, John Profumo had resigned, the Lord's Prayer had been banned in the American public schools." (*Couples*: 188) The one hopeful note in this plaint is that of Valentina Tereshkova, and even she seems somehow a woman who abandons the earth for something rarer and more treacherous. The Kennedy administration, fabled Camelot with its self-indulgence, erotic trouble, and inevitable grief, shadows the town of Tarbox as heaven shadows earth, but still it throws a shadow; indeed, the rumor of a too-handsome king and a wife who suffers the loss of her premature child with queenly restraint will find a closer echo in Ken and Foxy Whitman, who intrude—he "icy," she "arrogant"—into the closely bound circle of the older couples of Tarbox, whose society seems composed of inquisitive sex, affection, riddles, and regrets. It is a society in which virtually all connecting links are endangered, even those which have had the benefit of sacrament. The violent sense of regret following Foxy's abortion (for she conceives a child with Piet near the end of their affair), and the display of heavenly reproof which strikes the steeple of the Congregationalist church Piet sometimes attends seem aspects of a common failure to cherish "the link between," which it is the hero's business to forge between himself and the woman, as between himself and God.

One can risk a tentative equation. Confronted with the fractured certainties of Tarbox, the narration of *Couples* has become rather coolly matter-of-fact; the graver the sin, the defter the aphorism. It provokes a sometimes eerie tension: the lives of the couples do seem hauntingly fragile, while the narration often has the rectilinear, patient hopefulness of architectural blue-prints. Piet loves whomever he sleeps with; Updike loves whatever he draws. In *Couples*, things are drawn in detail, lives fitted into precise perspective:

> All houses, all things that enclosed, pleased Piet, but his modest Dutch sense of how much of the world he was permitted to mark off and hold was precisely satisfied by this flat lot two hundred feet back from the road, a mile

from the center of town, four miles distant from the sea. (*Couples*: 9)

Throughout the novel various settings, most exhaustively the houses of the couples, are blueprinted with this degree of earnest attention. Updike has a quick eye for idiosyncracies peculiar to the era and to the precise degree of disintegration within the marriage. Future museum curators will have, in *Couples*, a transparent treasury of diagrams from which a middle class household, New England, circa 1963, can be reconstructed:

The furnishings of the Saltzes' living room pressed in upon Foxy's emptiness: velvety dark easy chairs wearing doilies on their forearms, maple magazine racks of *Scientific American* and *Newsweek* and *Look*, inquisitive bridge lamps leaning over the chairs' left shoulders, Van Gogh sunning on the walls, wedding pictures frozen on the top of an upright piano with yellow teeth, an evil-footed coat-rack and a speckled oblong mirror in the dark foyer, narrow stairs plunging upward perilously, children climbing each night in a fight with fear. Her mother's Delaware second cousins had lived in such houses, built narrow to the street and lined with hydrangea bushes where a child could urinate or hide from her third cousins. The Jews have inherited the middle class—nobody else wants it. (*Couples*: 190)

Although the last observation is Foxy's, one assumes, because the narrative here is tracking her rather precarious frame of mind, the adjectival slant is Updike's—*evil-footed, speckled, narrow, dark*. The Saltzes' marriage is also to some degree narrow and dark. What light there is, they must hoard in order to deal with the consequences of adultery, each separate act of which is like a stone thrown into the calm pool of the couples: it causes rings, and the rings travel steadily outward from the

48

central vortex to the shadowy edges.

Couples is the most unabashedly aphoristic of Updike's novels. Marriage and sex elicit a thorny little bouquet:

> Every marriage is a hedged bet. (*Couples*: 48)

> Every marriage tends to consist of an aristocrat and a peasant. (*Couples*: 66)

> All love is a betrayal, in that it flatters life. The loveless man is best armed. (*Couples*: 54)

As if it were catching, the characters take turns at aphorism:

> "Resistability [in a man] is a direct function of the female decision to resist or not to." (*Couples*: 178)

> "I've never understood why people are so shocked when somebody sleeps with his best friend's wife. Obviously, his best friend's wife is the one he sees most *of*." (*Couples*: 138)

Updike's quality of wistfulness, of a puzzled sandpapering of the surfaces of the world, has here been replaced by a more carpentered prose in which the angles are right angles, the statements more often declarative than quizzical. That Cézanne-like tactic of grappling after "shade and shape," characteristic of *The Centaur*, the *Olinger Stories*, and *Rabbit, Run* is less in evidence here, although it never quite vanishes altogether. This new tone accords with the character of the hero, Piet, of whom his wife observes: "He likes to skate but isn't much of a swimmer. He thinks the sea is wasteful. I think *I* prefer things to be somewhat formless. Piet likes them finished." (*Couples*: 69)

No one can skate on the surface of the sea. *Couples* is a book about skaters, lives flashing across the fragile surfaces offered by the world. Piet—who is an orphan; who has already confronted death, and found it terrifying—is doubly vulnerable, a truly married man in love with adultery. Piet trusts domesticity, and longs for enclosure. Release for him is nearly unbearable. Once he and his wife have finally separated, the rift originating in Piet's various affairs, most crucially the one with Foxy Whitman, Piet stumbles into self-analysis in the classical method of heroes brooding by the sea:

> In his loneliness he detected companionship in the motion of waves, especially those distant waves lifting arms of spray along the bar, hailing him. The world was more Platonic than he had suspected. He found he missed friends less than friendship; what he felt, remembering Foxy, was a nostalgia for adultery itself—its adventure, the acrobatics its deceptions demand, the tensions of its hidden strings, the new landscapes it makes us master. (*Couples*: 450)

Nimbly, that last "us" draws us in: we are made to see Piet's truth, that acrobatics, removed from the precarious height of deception, become simply calisthentics; landscapes previously mastered tend to blur. No one can commit adultery without a wife.

Couples, tending inevitably toward this truth, follows the uncoupling of husbands and wives, including Piet and Angela; the uncoupling of God from the churches of Tarbox; the uncoupling of Piet's profession, construction, from stability of intent and grace of execution. This is a critical lapse when viewed in the light of Updike's enduring preoccupation with the learning of a trade. Piet has his trade, and within it he is capable of painstakingly fine work, yet honesty and symmetry seem to slip through his fingers. There is a reminiscence of Piet's fate in the Maples' story, "Gesturing": "They had known the contractor who built it, this mock antique wing, a dozen years ago, and then left town, bankrupt, disgraced, and oddly cheerful. His memory hovered between the beams."(*Too Far to Go*: 227) Finally, there is the uncoupling of those married pairs who are bound to each other, at the rather serene beginning of the novel, in what Freddy Thorne—to my mind Updike's most fabulously loathsome villain, full of spite and meddlesome obscenities, the devil domesticated into dentist—describes in a Greek chorus-like aside, quoted to Piet by his wife:

> "He's a jerk," she said carelessly, of Freddy Thorne. Her voice was lowered by the pressure of her chin against her chest; the downward reaching of her arms gathered her breasts to a dark crease. "But he talks about things that interest women. Food. Psychology. Children's teeth."
>
> "What does he say psychological?"
>
> "He was talking tonight about what we all see in each other."
>
> "Who?"
>
> "You know. Us. The couples."
>
> "What Freddy Thorne sees in me is a free drink. What he sees in you is a gorgeous fat ass."
>
> She deflected the compliment. "He thinks we're a circle. A magic circle of heads to keep the night out. He told me he gets frightened if he doesn't see us over the weekend. He thinks we've made a church of each other." (*Couples*: 12)

While the nominal compliment is of a sort characteristic of Updike's husbands—"simultaneous doses of honey and gall"— the list of "things that interest women" seems almost comically impoverished, the dialogue itself is pure post-party détente, full of smuggled erotic vigor. Undressing in the same room, Updike's men and women seem exposed to rare moments of revelation, like Adam and Eve astonished by shame. It is as if, to Updike's painterly eye, dishabille is a more fraught state than nakedness. Updike likes his characters in halfway states, and the partial vulnerability of poised undress triggers one of the Maples' fiercest quarrels, in the story "Eros Rampant":

> In the dim light he hardly knows this woman, her broken gestures, her hasty voice. Her silver slip glows and crackles as she wriggles into a black knit cocktail dress; with a kind of determined agitation she paces around the bed, to the bureau and back. As she moves, her body seems to be gathering bulk from the shadows, bulk and a dynamic elasticity. (*Too Far to Go*: 134)

In the scene above, Joan Maple is moved to a confession of infidelity; here is Piet, spurred to accusatory panic by his wife's undress:

> Having unclasped her party pearls, Angela pulled her dress, the black decollete knit, over her head. Its soft wool caught in her hairpins. As she struggled, lamplight struck zigzag fire from her slip and static electricity made its nylon adhere to her flank. The slip lifted, exposing stocking-tops and garters. Without her head she was all form, sweet, solid.
>
> Pricked by love, he accused her: "You're not happy with me." (*Couples*: 11)

If it were not for the apprehensive accuracy of this description—the deftness of "zigzag fire" and the affectionate domestic sound of "flank" instead of "hip" or "thigh," as well as the insistence of *full, sweet, solid*—one might conclude only that Updike tends to admire women removing black cocktail dresses. The opposition—between form and airiness, shadow-buttressed nakedness and fallen cloth—is almost an Edenic one. The black knit is removed to show a white slip, and the revelation of a silky white inner garment has something about it of the revelation of innocence, original and shy. The black dress, recently shed, signalled a seduction directed outward, toward the world. In "Gesturing," the sparring, separated Maples go out for a dinner which already feels, to Richard, "illicit."

> Richard rose from his supplicant position, relieved to hear Joan coming down the stairs. She was dressed to go out, in the timeless black dress with the scalloped neckline, and a collar of Mexican silver. He was wary. He must be wary. They had had it. They must have had it. (*Too Far to Go*: 227)

In the novel *Couples*, however, the balance of anxiety centers around who is undressing whom, rather than what happens during the undressing. Almost everyone is undressing someone. Freddy Thorne's remark that the couples form "a magic circle of heads to keep the night out" has a ring of augury. It sounds child-like, this magical task, and it is; it sounds playful, and is almost certainly not. The couples often appear as children about to be reprimanded by a mysterious source. This source is omniscient, and no more paternally indulgent than Piet when he demands, of Angela: " 'Why shouldn't children suffer? They're supposed to suffer. How else can they learn to be good?' For he felt that if only in the matter of suffering he knew more than she, and that without him she would raise their daughters as she had been raised, to live in a world that didn't exist." (*Couples*: 13)

In the real world, the world that does exist, the premonition of loss—the possibility of disastrous failure inherent in the erotic quest—can narrow a life, but the couples of Tarbox experiment with dangerous things as if they possessed a child-like immunity to consequence, as if what they did were only playing, and play— an insular realm, necessary to development, rich in improvisation and internal constraint, but beyond the formal grammar of morality by which "real life" is ordered—should not have weakened the bonds between them. The couples slip in and out of adulthood, their own children sometimes literally shuffled from bed to bed to make way for the trysts of their parents. In hint, in metaphor, in their dialogue, the couples are slantingly revealed as, truly, children themselves:

> "What do you and Freddy find to talk about for hours on end? You huddle in the corner like children playing jacks." (*Couples*: 11)

> Like a rebuked child Foxy entered the living room; its human brightness seemed strange. (*Couples*: 189)

> [Ben Saltz's] wounded love of Carol weighed on the air of the room and gave the couples an agitated importance, like that of children in safe from a thunderstorm. (*Couples*: 240)

> Her lips were forced apart over clenched teeth like a child's after swimming and, touched and needing to touch her, Piet asked, "Why are you being such a bitch tonight?" (*Couples*: 245)

If suffering fosters goodness in a child, then Piet—orphan, saddened husband, chastened adulterer—should end by being very, very good, but in *Couples*, that isn't the way things work. Dread tips the balance. Piet, as an unmarried man, freed from the dread of discovery, is strangely null. The original dread—the one that causes exile from the garden—has to do with nakedness and fear of discovery, and Adam tries—in a conversational, if ineffective, way—to circumvent it. Angela Hanema undresses in her closet, presumably so that her husband cannot observe her. He kicks the closet door; it is the first act of domestic violence in *Couples*, and it echoes the first one in Eden.

> . . . Piet, suffocated by an obscure sense of exclusion, seeking to obtain at least the negotiable asset of a firm

> rejection, . . . hopped across the hearth-bricks worn like a passageway in Delft and sharply kicked shut Angela's closet door, nearly striking her. She was naked. (*Couples*: 14)

Angela and Piet are Adam and Eve, mutually exposed and mutually fearful, who have egged each other on and gotten in trouble. Awareness dawns in the half-light and sheltering right angles of Piet's beloved bedroom. Already, within the first chapter, there is an elegiac note; for this couple, nothing will ever quite be the same, although Angela will remain a shy and rather anxious Eve to Piet's clumsily made, and clumsily male, Adam. The descriptions of the two have something painterly about them, a grave Renaissance richness.

> He too was naked. Piet's hands, feet, and genitals were those of a larger man, as if his maker, seeing that the cooling body had been left too small, had injected a final surge of plasma which at these extremities had ponderously clotted. Physically he held himself, his tool-toughened palms curved and his acrobat's back a bit bent, as if conscious of a potent burden. (*Couples*: 14)

Reading "potent burden," one guesses—if this is Adam, the burden must be guilt. In contrast to Piet's Adam, Angela's Eve seems a more thoughtful, and a far more consciously crafted, presence, as if God got her right on the first try:

> Angela had flinched and now froze, one arm protecting her breasts. A luminous polleny pallor, the shadow of that summer's bathing suit, set off her surprisingly luxurious pudenda. The slack forward cant of her belly remembered her pregnancies. Her legs were varicose. But her tipped arms seemed, simple and symmetrical, a maiden's; her white feet were high-arched and neither little toe touched

the floor. Her throat, wrists, and triangular bush appeared the pivots for some undeniable effort of flight, but like Eve on a portal she crouched in shame, stone. (*Couples*: 14)

When Updike describes Piet as awkward suitor of Angela, it is as if the writer of Genesis had chosen, in an unlikely aside, to document this aboriginal wooing in its green and silent context: "Their courtship passed as something instantly forgotten, like an enchantment, or a mistake." Against the crossweave of irony and image, the sentence rings wonderfully apt. "Time came unstuck. . . . Her father, a wise-smiling man in a gray-tailored suit, failed to disapprove." They live, as did Adam and Eve, in a realm of fertility which is in itself magical. "The Hanema's first child, a daughter, was born nine months after the wedding night." And when Updike observes, "Nine years later Piet still felt, with Angela, a superior power seeking through her to employ him," one imagines that the superior power is, subtly, God.

Adam and Eve are at a loss outside the garden; Tarbox is somehow the exemplary milieu in which to *be* at a loss. The very streets are named for antique virtues. The landscape of narrow islands and brimming fawn-colored marshes stretching to the sea is formally seductive, the ring of couples informally, but nonetheless expertly, so. Each exudes some secret scent of uneasiness. "Piet felt, brave small Dutch boy, a danger hanging tidal above his friends, in this town. . . . The men had stopped having careers and the women had stopped having babies. Liquor and love were left." (*Couples*: 17) In spite of certain lyrical—tender and scholarly—passages which deal exactingly with fellatio and gin, in *Couples* liquor and love will stand revealed as inadequate panacea; this ring of heads can't keep out the dark. Piet knows this. His instinct is to stick his finger into the hole in the dam, and patiently wait. There is something of the foiled crusader, the not-unwillingly stymied martyr, about Piet. As hero he alternates between brave attempts at reckoning with dread—he seems to feel most at ease, most successful at fending off death and disorder, in the wake of orgasm, as if each woman he makes love to renders up to him a measure of light and sudden harmony, a glimpse, at least, of the grail—and cold recognition of the simple biological stubbornness of those things, mortality and entropy, that he fears. It is possible that death is more guileless in its approach to the hero, more pliantly seductive, than even sex. On Indian Hill, site of a series of tract houses whose construction Piet somewhat reluctantly supervises, he discovers a bone:

> "Cow bone," Leon said.
> "Doesn't it seem too delicate?"
> "Deer?"
> "Don't they say there was an Indian burying ground somewhere on this south side?" (*Couples*: 91)

And the very slenderness of the bone—"Isn't it too delicate?"—and the way that it catches the eye and then fails to properly haunt the mind—for in the end Piet simply drops it, with no more ceremony that someone discarding a torn movie ticket—remain with him. "Embarrassed, Piet said, 'Well, keep your eyes open. We may be on sacred ground.'" Piet, in his guise of hero, does keep his eyes open, and tensely attends to the sacredness, not only of the ground, but of the revelations of his lovers. The clumsy amalgam of his body reflects this tension: his hands and feet and genitals, for building and running and making love, are those of "a larger man." That Piet, who is so in love with the virtues of symmetry, should be himself so unsymmetrical, is a glintingly uneasy irony.

But uneasiness makes novels, and *Couples* is richer for it. Other ironies surface, some startling. There are premonitions of feminism deep in the heart of Tarbox, almost the last place one would have expected it. Piet is nullified by the separation from his wife; the only context in which his tensions acquire meaning and drama has been eroded. Angela seems correspondingly lightened and loosened, until within the system of erotic checks-and-balances by which the couples operate, she is an unknown quantity, free, highly charged, spectacular as an electron newly chipped from an atom.

> Once, driving past it, the old Robinson house, Piet thought it was fortunate he and Angela had not bought it, for it had proved to be an unlucky house; then realized they had shared in its bad luck anyway. In his solitude he was growing absent-minded. He noticed a new woman down-town—that elastic proud gait announcing education, a spirit freed from the peasant shuffle, arms swinging, a sassy ass, trim ankles. Piet hurried along the other side of Charity Street to get a glimpse of her front and found, just before she turned into the savings bank, that the woman was Angela. (*Couples*: 450)

Angela's complaint occurs earlier in the novel, before she and Piet have quite come undone:

> I'm not on anybody's wavelength. Not even the children's, now that Nancy's no longer a baby. I'm very alone, Piet . . . I really don't seem to be quite *here*; that's why I meant it about psychiatry. I think I need a rather formal kind of help. I need to go to a school where the subject is myself. (*Couples*: 380)

Certainly the sound is of intimate personal grievance, but there is an edginess in Angela's voice which foreshadows—however diffidently; angels are diffident creatures—the balance of the following decade, in which just such complaints would be broadcast as parables. It would be wrong to read too much into Angela's protest, or to view too optimistically her "proud elastic gait" after the loss of Piet (one suspects that much of this new springiness is simply relief, that Piet's quarrels with himself and with the world had reduced her to exhaustion), but it is one of the real strengths of Updike's affectionate and complex portrait of Angela that she should, however roughly, sketch the possibility for a philosophy so alien to him, to Angela, even to the realm of Tarbox.

Piet is of a sufficiently heroic disposition to suffer in an un-childlike way at the wrongs that are done between them, but he suffers most credibly at the hands of the world, rather than of his wife. "Piet, hammer in hand, likes to feel the bite taken into gravity. The upright weight-bearing was a thing his eye would see, and a house never looked as pretty again to him as it did in the framing, before bastard materials and bastard crafts eclipsed honest carpentry, and work was replaced by delays and finagling with sub-contractors—electricians like weasels, grubby plumbers, obdurate motionless masons." (*Couples*: 206) And so Piet, in love, loves best the "framing" of an affair, the innocent and airy state where the lovers are mutually independent, where no emotion is so literal it cannot be revoked. He abandons his first lover, Georgene Thorne, in the wake of what seems a negligible difficulty, the first serious hint that the world will intrude into the sunniness of their sex, set within the "post-pill paradise."

> She possessed, this conscientious clubwoman and firm mother, a lovely unexpected gift. Her sexuality was guileless. As formed by the first years of her marriage with Freddy, it had the directness of eating, the ease of running. Her insides were innocent. (*Couples*: 58)

The guilelessness draws him in. Trouble daunts him, though, and Piet finishes this affair in evasive discourtesy. He seems happiest with Foxy Whitman, his second lover, while their affair is still sketchy, none of the outlines blurred by bastard considerations. Their affair is conducted within the house Angela has coveted, and its scent is the honest, even holy, one of wood shavings and new paint, for the house is being rebuilt, with Piet as contractor, for the pregnant Foxy and her icy husband, who commutes to his laboratory in Boston. This house is the tangent against which the arc of the affair rests. Piet and Foxy's lovemaking draws its rhythm from the echo of hammerstrokes; they are firm and astonished and absorbed, as a carpenter is absorbed by the quirks in the grain of the wood, by each other's hungers and oddities. The completion of the house coincides with Piet's attempt to end the affair, an attempt spurred in part by the birth of Foxy's child, a boy. Foxy's husband has never posed any serious threat to Piet's ascendancy; Piet assumes that her son inevitably will. In a sense, Piet is trying to leave Foxy in good hands, with a life that has narrowly skirted ruin, in a house that he has altered to fit her whims. The affair proves strangely tenacious; Foxy seems more stricken and awkward than he, and, almost in defiance of Piet's finely administered distance from her, she conceives a child by him. It has always seemed odd to me that anyone would accuse Updike's work of lacking violence, for the abortion which follows is so very violent—spooky in its quality of removal and enforced silence, and in the possibility of mortal danger—that it sucks expectancy and hope from the very air these characters breathe.

> Not until days later . . . did Piet learn, not from Freddy but from her as told to her by Freddy, that at the moment of anesthesia [Foxy] had panicked; she had tried to strike the Negress pressing the sweet, sweet mask to her face and through the first waves of ether had continued to cry that she should go home, that she was supposed to have this baby, that the child's father was coming to smash the door down with a hammer and would stop them.(*Couples*: 397)

Queerly, the abortion is an act of desperation sufficient to wrench Piet from his hero's course, from woman to woman to woman. His course will be altered: from wife to lover to lover to wife, with the second wife, Foxy, already promising trouble. In a sense, the one thing Piet cannot embrace is complexity. Skater rather than swimmer, carpenter instead of grubby plumber, Piet has maintained throughout his adventures a workmanlike erotic innocence. He is oddly unsullied; he drops bones back to the earth where he found them; he leaves his lovers to fashion their own solutions, as if he had served his proper function as a temporary catalyst, the flame below the flask. When Georgene observes that "only Piet had brought her word of a world where vegetation was heraldic and every woman was some man's queen," she fails to comprehend that Piet's duty, bringing the word, renders his attentions to any one woman peculiarly finite. Later, confronted with Foxy and Piet rather calmly conversing, she is forced to bite down hard on her own jealousy, and tells them, ". . . Maybe the rest of us are poisoned and you two upset us with your innocence." This has the quality of an announcement: Piet and Foxy *have* come to a sort of conclusion. "They were lordly, in perfect control. Having coaxed the abortion from their inferiors, they were quite safe, and would always exist for each other." (*Couples*: 404)

The novel ends, and Piet and Foxy end, by being married, which is not quite the same as being safe. There remains the troubling ring of Foxy's question to Piet, in a letter she writes from St. Croix, the island which selters her during the interval of her divorce from Ken. *"The question is, should I (or the next woman, or the next) subdue you into marriage? How much more generous it would be to let you wander, and suffer—there are so few wanderers left . . . When you desire to be the world's husband, what right do I have to make you my own?"*

Bech: A Bachelor

HENRY BECH OUGHT TO BE THE MAN TO PUT THESE
theories to the proof. The unknowns by which an Updike hero is
tested—the vagaries of adultery, the insights born of stealth—
are as remote to Bech as the moon, or Russia. He practices a
perservering and frugal bachelorhood unique in Updike's writ-
ings. It is impossible to imagine Bech, in the bewildered way of
the hero of the short story "Problems," laboring home from a
laundromat with an armful of wet laundry slowly dampening his
chest. Bech would have let his dirty clothes accumulate beneath
his bed, washed them in his bathroom sink, and laid them out to
dry on a slightly dusty radiator—where his socks, paired with his
mistress's, do dry, in the story "Bech Panics." If domesticity
poses any problems for Bech, they are problems that can be
solved, and therefore, in Updike's lexicon, not really problems at
all. Bech could hardly be farther from Lowell's description of an
unmarried man as a "turtle without a shell," for there is nothing
blinkingly quiescent, and very little which seems vulnerable,
about Bech. He handles his apprehensions more ingeniously
than a turtle, with its methodically compact program of retreat,
is allowed to. Bech can evade, invade, invent, outwit, lie, scheme,
fly, betray. All of these methods are foreign to the humble

members of *Chelonia*. Bech is more exactly located within the genus *Rattus*, as he himself observes. He exercises a rat's prerogatives, chief among them a cleverly preserved solitude, a virtuoso memory for rotten smells, a rather small number of erotic scruples, and an unfailing lightness on his feet.

> . . . he tried to explain his peculiar status, not as a lion, with a lion's confining burden of symbolic portent, but as a graying, furtively stylish rat permitted to gnaw and roam behind the wainscoting of a firetrap about to be demolished anyway. . . . (*Bech: A Book*: 15)

The simile is an extended play on Bech's brief companionship with the Russian literary lions, Vosnesensky and Yevtushenko. Updike himself has translated some of Yevtushenko's work, including the title poem of the volume *Stolen Apples*, sufficiently erotic and sly and wonderful to have moved Bech himself. The "firetrap about to be demolished anyway" would, in the logic of the simile, be the thinnish facade of American fiction, earlier abandoned by Bech's compatriots "H. Roth, D. Fuchs, and J. Salinger." Bech could be right to feel that contemporary fiction, for him, is a firetrap. His own fire—in the common dictum equating fire and creativity—is certainly trapped.

Other Updike heroes have been alone, but none deliberately sought the state; it fell to them through accident or sorrow. Hook was solitary within the baffled and inquisitive company of the poorhouse, but that was the fault of deafness and an archaic reserve in his manner. Chiron, in *The Centaur*, was lonely because of the hybrid state into which he was born. Chiron could only remain restlessly aloof from students and deities alike; courted by a goddess, he proved himself less shy than politic. Bech's bachelorhood strikes me as a state the Centaur could have envied, somewhere deep within his obedient heart. The economy of means—Bech has lived "for twenty years in a grim if roomy Riverside Drive apartment building"—coupled with the pervasiveness of erotic adventure, and the possibility of subsequent male thoughtfulness, might have pleased the Centaur as they clearly please Bech. Both Chiron and Bech are teachers, though Bech only briefly, in the story "Bech Panics," but the reverence of his nubile students evokes and echoes that of the Centaur's pupils. Even their fates—Bech's wistfully endured, Chiron's granted him by Zeus—are heroically parallel.

> Zeus had loved his old friend, and lifted him up, and set him among the stars in the constellation Sagittarius. Here, in the Zodiac, now above, now below the horizon, he assists in the regulation of our destinies, though in this latter time few living mortals cast their eyes respectfully toward heaven, and fewer still sit as students to the stars. (*The Centaur*: 222)

> Bech tried to clear his vision by contemplating the back of the heads [of the famous]. They were blank: blank shabby backs of a cardboard tableau lent substance only by the credulous, by old women and children. His knees trembled, as if after an arduous climb. He had made it, he was here, in Heaven. Now what? (*Bech: A Book*: 186)

Interestingly, these are the two clearest personal approximations of immortality you find within Updike's work, where the hunger for eternal life has tormented his heroes since the crisis of belief in the short story "Pigeon Feathers." If Bech seems less at ease in Heaven than Chiron, it is because he has not endured the hybrid tensions which the Centaur, in spite of himself, suffered nobly on earth. Bech is of a whole, and wholes are—at least in Updike's work—less sacred than fragments. Thus, one hero appropriates a constellation, and the other merely an empty chair.

Updike's work, as we have seen, determinedly chronicles

problems, divisions, declines—a pageantry in which the costumes are coming unstitched. Updike is interested, not only in the instant of unstitching, but in the exact stresses imposed on threads before they fray. He is fond of linking domestic security with adulterous danger, erotic gains with emotional losses. Without the imminence of a dangerous rift, his heroes would seem to be treading a tightrope suspended only inches above the ground. This is what Bech, rather adroitly, manages to do; he carries the performance off with irony, a pantomimed willingness to see himself as absurd, and a sense of balance more finely developed that his circumstances call for, but the truth is that Bech, unlike Updike's other heroes, never seems to be in very serious danger. As an unbeliever and an unmarried man, he hasn't got far to fall. His desperation is never silhouetted against a void sufficiently black. When he observes the state of his own soul—and as an introspective Jewish bachelor with time on his hands, he talks to himself more often than to anyone else, certainly more often than he talks to any actual woman—he frames his observations in lists. Bech *itemizes.* His daydreams are loaded with facts, numerals, directions, and street names, like a pseudo-autobiography given to a spy to be memorized, and then swallowed. He doesn't just think of his gradeschool; he thinks of ". . . P.S. 87, on West Seventy-seventh Street and Amsterdam Avenue." He doesn't remember himself as a child walking down a block; he remembers ". . . a mock-Tudor apartment house like some evilly enlarged and begrimed fairy-tale chalet . . . to Broadway and Seventy-ninth and the IRT kiosk with its compounded aroma of hot brakes, warm bagels, and vomit." (*Bech*: 172) He is probably the only Updike hero, amid a thousand incantatory evocations of the reek of lilacs and the musk of women, who ever smells bagels.

Bech's Jewish past is described as "neglected," but the neglect is not precisely attributed to him. One imagines, through Bech, Updike's neglect, though whenever Jewishness is touched upon the writing assumes an apologetic quality, half cultural documentary and half unassimilated rue. When Bech speaks of Jews as a group he uses the pronoun *they*, rather than the more obvious choice, *we*. "I think the Jewish feeling," Bech says, "is that wherever they happen to be, it's rather paradisiacal, because they're there." (*Bech*: 17) It is as if *we* would not have been quite accurate. *They* is safer, and stranger, given Bech's presumed Jewishness. That there is a patchwork, piecemeal, improvised quality to this Jewishness, Bech engagingly protests:

> At first blush, for example, in Bulgaria (eclectic sexuality, bravura narcissim, thinning curly hair), I sound like some gentlemanly Norman Mailer; then that London glimpse of *silver* hair glints more of gallant, glamorous Bellow, the King of the Leprechauns, than of stolid old yours truly. My childhood seems out of Alex Portnoy and my ancestral past out of I. B. Singer. I get a whiff of Malamud in your city breezes, and am I paranoid to feel my "block" an ignoble version of the more or less noble renunciations of H. Roth, D. Fuchs, and J. Singer? Withal, something Waspish, theological, sacred, and insinuatingly ironical that derives, my wild surmise is, from you. (*Bech*: v)

The *you* named in this passage is Updike, for this is a letter Bech has written to him, one of the numerous Nabokovian doublings-back the book contains. Even Bech's literary resume has the look of scissors-and-paste pastiche. His early, funny stories—"Stree-raight'n Yo' Shoulduhs, Boy!", in *Liberty*—about a Jew uneasily bivouacked among Gentiles—can't help evoking J. D. Salinger's "For Esmé—with Love and Squalor," although Bech seems to have had something less errantly tender in mind. His career in fact sounds serpentine enough to have brushed all the touchstones of chic: "His first novel, *Travel Light*, had become a minor classic of the fifties. . . . His second novel, a lyrical gesture of disgust, novella-length, called *Brother Pig*, did his reputation no harm and cleared his brain, he

67

thought, for a frontal assault on the wonder of life. The assault, surprisingly, consumed five years, in which his mind and work habits developed in circles, or loops, increasingly leisurely and whimsical; when he sat down at his desk, for instance, his younger self, the somehow fictitious author of his earlier fictions, seemed to be not quite displaced, so that he became an uneasy, blurred composite, like the image left on film by too slow an exposure." (*Bech*: 133) This is a description to be examined carefully: the word *frontal*, pertaining not only to assault but to certain lobes of the brain, perhaps contains the germ of Bech's unease. He assaults life with more mind than spirit; he is more sergeant than pilgrim. The prim phrase "too slow an exposure," implying as it does that the amount of existing light has been underestimated, contains a nuance of professorly disapproval. Light is important in Updike's work—where it comes from, and how much there is. Bech's technique, not only in writing but in existing, is plagued by such lapses of attention. In another Nabokov-like twist, this "somehow fictitious author" is exactly that—this is a fiction hàunting a fiction *within* a fiction. Enough? Not quite, it seems. Throughout the short stories of *Bech: A Book*, the voice of an invisible instructor, ill-tempered and vengeful but sharp-eyed ("I saw you, in the back row, glancing at your wristwatch, and don't think that glance will sweeten your term grade. . . ." [*Bech*: 19]), scrapes through the text now and then, in a dour echo to the chorus of overlapping personae characteristic of Nabokov's novels. This lecturer ought logically to be Updike himself—Bech's letter is addressed to him as the author of "this little *jeu* of a book"—but he sounds distinctly unlike the Updike of television interviews, essays, reviews, or *New Yorker* "Notes and Comments." This instructor's voice is much more slantingly similar to the tone of mocking, elaborately gentle pedantry in Nabokov's *Lectures on Literature*. The peculiar care which the lecturer lavishes on Bech's borrowed campus bedroom in "Bech Panics," would not embarrass the man who diagrammed Gregor Samsa's flat. The elaborately constructed appendices recall *Pale Fire* in the splicing of the real with the highly improbable. This is a book, narrated by an alter ego, about a Doppelgänger.

> [Bech] was an Aristotelian and not a Platonist. Write him down, if [the interviewer] must write him down as something, as a disbeliever; he disbelieved in the Pope, in the Kremlin, in the Vietcong, in the American eagle, in astrology, in Arthur Schlesinger, Eldridge Cleaver, Senator Eastland, and Eastman Kodak. Nor did he believe overmuch in his disbelief. (*Bech*: 158)

Bech is an Aristotelian emotionally as well as philosophically. His affection turns toward small, specific things; the mathematics of his heart is conducted in fractions more often than whole numbers. In this regard for the narrow, the exact and the momentary, he is not unlike Updike's other heroes: Piet Hanema in *Couples* also declares himself an Aristotelian. It is an important distinction for an Updike hero to make, and it carries along with it a coded burden of rectitude, like the names Barth or Kierkegaard—these are holy words in an extremely personal lexicon, and Updike's writing loosens and breathes with something like relief whenever they are summoned. Aristotelianism, however, remains the sole tenet of the hero's creed to which Bech subscribes. Disbelief tends to mark Updike's villains, most notably Freddy Thorne and Richard Mathias. Wives, as in *Marry Me* and *A Month of Sundays*, are reproved for doubting too much. So disbelief rests rather tensely and strangely on the shoulders of a hero, but Bech is Jewish, and his righteousness therefore of a chromosomal and inevitable kind; the hook in his nose hymns for him.

Neither does he attempt to fix the wit of erotic insight into the wisdom of married love. His heartaches, occuring in rather rapid succession, balance one another out like the opposing ends of a long and delicate equation. He does not confront the great polarity—*x* and *y*, wife and lover—which baffles Updike's other heroes. Bech has, instead of a great love, several medium-good ones. Even when he falls in love in London, in the story "Bech Swings?", the quality of this love is remedial rather than risky.

> It was his charm and delusion to see women as dieties—idols whose jewel was set not in the center of their foreheads but between their legs, with another between their lips, and pairs more sprinkled up and down, from ankles to eyes, the length of their adorable, alien forms.... But perhaps, Bech thought, one more woman, one more leap would bring him safe into the high calm pool of immortality where Proust and Hawthorne and Catullus float, glassy-eyed and belly-up. (*Bech*: 135)

Bech never does devote much of his normally inquisitive energy to determining what might lie behind a woman's forehead; it could be for this reason that his loves share a quality of interchangeability. All jewels are alike in the dark. The single woman Bech approaches with some interest in her peculiar character is the poet in the short story "The Bulgarian Poetess," and even she is granted only the sketchiest of backgrounds and the slightest possible prowess in English:

> "Your poems. Are they difficult?" [Bech says]
> "They are difficult—to write." [she says]
> "But not to read?"
> "I think—not so very."
> "Good. Good." (*Bech*: 59)

The language barrier ensures the distance between them; Bech does not need to construct his own discreetly melancholy defenses. Precariousness is guaranteed by their situation, so neither of them needs to invent it. Bech seems more candid than usual, more *present* on the page, and the inscription with which he ends the story is beautifully straightforward. It is difficult, if not impossible, to tell why a short story is beautiful, but for me the success of "The Bulgarian Poetess" lies in that emotional détente, in the vulnerability, however brief, of an often very guarded man.

Still, the weightiest negative which characterizes Bech is his writer's block. Almost alone among Updike's heroes, he is famous, but he is prevented from the practice of his trade—and the practice of a trade is crucial to the psyche of heroes. Bech's failure is inexplicably unredeemed by sorrow; his manner of thinking about this enormous absence in the center of his life seems curiously blithe. Sorrow itself, throughout Updike's work, has sometimes seemed a profession—it has its practitioners, among them Chiron in The Centaur and Joey's mother in *Of the Farm*, and its wages in patience and insight, and it can keep a man's hands full. Bech's hands are as empty as his Russian suitcase is imperiously stuffed. The truth is that most of Updike's errant heroes, throughout all of their various trials and tribulations, show up at work every single day. In Bech, Updike seems to be debating the virtues of intelligent impotence. When Bech conceives the idea for a novel to be entitled *Think Big*, it is the bigness you sense—an airy inflation—rather than the thinking. "... it was a big book, he saw, with a blue jacket of coated stock and his unsmiling photo full on the back, bled top and bottom...." (*Bech*: 157) "Bled top and bottom" bleaches the image of vigor. Updike himself conceives of his novels as rather precise geometric shapes, so the process may not be altogether foreign:

> I really begin with some kind of solid, coherent image, some notion of the shape of the book and even of its texture. *The Poorhouse Fair* was meant to have a sort of Y shape. *Rabbit, Run* was a kind of zig-zag. *The Centaur* was sort of a sandwich. I can't begin until I know the beginning and have some sense of what's going to happen between

[sic]. (*Picked-Up Pieces*: 481)

Without work, Bech has fallen from the one sort of grace available to him. He approaches those touchstones of Updikean middle age—sleepless nights; a *crise* of the spirit; an increasingly ominous sense of his own mortality—but he seems to be carrying a tourist's Nikon rather than a pilgrim's seashell. On erotic ground, too, he is a tourist rather than worshipper, wondering what it would have felt like to wear a hair shirt. His knowledge of women's bodies is photographic rather than intimate; his affairs are public—chronicled in gossip columns, making the rounds of literary circles—and inconsequential to the degree that the adultery of a hero is private and riddled with premonitions of disaster. Bech grieves over his lack of children as if this were a tribal obligation on which he has defaulted, but his nostalgia for what-could-have-been remains nostalgia, and never escalates into hunger.

How can he be a hero if he is not hungry? For Bech, the quest into the erotic terrain of a particular woman has been circumvented by travels into countries which are literally foreign, and metaphorically feminine. Russia, wily and complex, is "the only country in the world you can be homesick for while you're still in it." (*Bech*: 19) Nostalgia for a woman's body, and the equating of that body with land, is a recurring theme in Updike's work, so this homesickness has an almost sexual intensity. The women in Bech's fiction seem to Bech's translator ". . . coldly observed. As if extraterrestrial life." (*ibid.*) Bech has failed to make the crucial connection between women and earth. He ventures into the interiors of real continents, instead of mythic ones. When Bech is introduced to the Bulgarian translator of *Alice in Wonderland*, the translator describes Carroll's work as "A marvellous book. . . . It truly takes us into another dimension. Something that must be done. We live in a new cosmos." (*Bech:* 57) This "something that must be done" is Bech's invisible obligation. A hero, willingly or not, should breach other dimensions, and the dimensions should be those of a beloved other, a woman, the mystery confined in skin.

Satori and Philodendrons:
Rabbit, Run

"IT HAS NEVER OCCURRED TO ME TO FACE THE terror but/as to how to hide from it I'm a virtual booth of information," A. R. Ammons wrote in the long poem *Sphere: The Form of a Motion*. A parallel line of reasoning—if not a comparably introspective mockery, for Rabbit is Updike's creature, rather than a variant of his self—is pursued in the novel *Rabbit, Run*. The book is a record of the evasive maneuvers practiced by Harry Angstrom, nicknamed Rabbit, the hero of a life gone formidably wrong. The thing that he wishes to hide from is exactly the kind of terror—darkness, death, the decay of awareness and possibility—that the world relentlessly sends his way. Rabbit's chief certainty in *Rabbit, Run* is that *it* is right behind him, breathing down the back of his neck.

Even Rabbit's name acknowledges that he is, however unwittingly, an example, linking error and expiation as inevitably as any character in Beatrix Potter. According to the *Random House Dictionary*, an angstrom is "a unit of length, equal to one tenth of a millimicron; or one ten millionth of a millimeter, primarily used to express electromagnetic wavelengths." Crucial, in this definition, is not only the fact that a unit of measurement so astonishingly small exists, but that it exists to

measure both the invisible—radio waves, x-rays, gamma rays—
and the spectrum of light edging boldly toward the visible, for
Rabbit's eyes "turn toward the light however it glances into his
retina." (*Rabbit, Run*: 219) Rabbit is an instrument by which
certain invisible forces—the willingness to seek the good; the
desire to run, to err, to reconcile—can be judged, as well as some
very visible things—the desertion of a wife; domestic ugliness
and disorder; alcoholic sorrow following hard on the heels of
adultery. Because he is always more than an instrument,
however, Rabbit remains scaldingly aware of the electricity that
runs through him, of the light that aches in the receptive cells of
the eye. Long after the publication of *Rabbit, Run*, when he was
discussing the Rabbit novels in an interview with John Callaway, Updike could speak of Rabbit's vulnerability to perception:
". . . his stream of consciousness, as it moves through these events
which are squalid and disastrous—as real events often are—[is]
nevertheless . . . a kind of praise-singing to the created world."
(*John Callaway Interviews*: 13)

In the opening pages of the novel, Rabbit is wearing a sign of
this vulnerability, the equivalent of his heart on his sleeve. "He
wonders if he should remove the Demonstrator badge from his
lapel but decides he will wear the same suit tomorrow. He has
only two, not counting a dark blue that is too hot for this time of
year." (*Rabbit, Run*: 13) This dark suit will figure in a grim way
late in the novel, when Rabbit wears it to the funeral of his infant
daughter. "He opens the closet door as far as he can without
bumping the television set and reaches far in and unzips a plastic
zippered storage bag and takes out his blue suit, a winter suit
made of wool, but the only dark one he owns." (*Rabbit, Run*:
261) It is still too hot for the suit—Rabbit's daughter was
drowned on the summer solstice, and the funeral follows two
days after—but the original mention of the suit, and the way it is
retrieved, rather fearfully and ceremoniously, from a dark closet
in the apartment where the death occurred, provides one of those

pairings by which the novel is structured. It *is* a beautifully structured work, as full of machinations, premonitions, and pitfalls as a fairy tale, yet balanced by unexpected symmetries of sound and incident. Updike's accounting of Rabbit's life has been so exact that the reader not only immediately recognizes the contents of the closet, but knows something of the sour resentment Rabbit must feel at this, the sullen winter cloth worn to a summer burial.

Within a page of this first mention of the Demonstrator badge pinned to his lapel, Rabbit's wife Janice demands petulantly, "What are you doing, becoming a saint?" Though she could easily be the last to recognize it, sainthood is indeed one of the possibilities inherent in Rabbit's skittish progress through the world. His travails are those of the heart, and he suffers them with a heated purity. He runs from circumstances, never from his own emotions, which have acquired—when so much in his life is cheap and disordered—a value equivalent to that of the Krugerrands in *Rabbit Is Rich*. Emotions are the coin of Rabbit's realm, his only earthly good, his single clue: "He hates all the people in the street in dirty everyday clothes, advertising their belief that the world arches over a pit, that death is final, that the wandering thread of his feelings leads nowhere." (*Rabbit, Run*: 217) With whim as the *modus operandi* of sainthood, Rabbit charts his erratic course. He considers himself one of the elect, and tends to admire the nervous spontaneity of his own heart, no matter what chaos comes of his acts—that is the world's fault, not his. Late in the novel, during an argument with his lover, Rabbit finds that the "way she is fighting for control of herself repels him; he doesn't like people who manage things. He likes things to happen of themselves." (*Rabbit, Run*: 281) In an earlier quarrel with his wife, when he is about leave her for the second time, she voices a demand that seems, although irritable, just, and he replies according to his creed.

▌   "Why can't you try to imagine how I *feel*? I've just had a baby."

"I can. I can but I don't want to, it's not the thing, the thing is how *I* feel. And I feel like getting out." (*Rabbit, Run*: 230)

In this—the italicized, anxiously forward-tilting *I*—Rabbit is most purely himself, and most purely a hero, however slender the thread that stretches ahead of him, however brutal the "things that happen of themselves."

In *Rabbit, Run* even language itself seems secretly anxious, as if confronting some fear it can neither precisely counter nor entirely evade. There is an almost placatory reliance on certain words—placatory in the sense that a prayer is placatory, and in the sense that any rhythm is, at some level, an attempt to stave off uncertainty, to fortify oneself against those things in the world that are frighteningly arbitrary. Still, these words recur with an insistence that is puzzlingly uncharacteristic of Updike's work, usually so wide-open to any fortuitous linguistic intrusion, so spirited and mobile, with a willingness to absorb the colloquial cadence, the exact names of streets and numbers of houses, the verbal *objet trouvé*—in short, whatever is at once peculiar and apt. "You spend so much of your own energy avoiding repeating yourself," the psychiatrist in the short story "The Fairy Godfathers" tells the perplexed hero; the observation seems to apply to Updike, the craftsman, as well. He once admired Mark Twain's use of the word "scatteration" for its spur-of-the-moment exactness, and he himself has resorted to such curiosities as "jubilating" and "centaurine" with the ease born of immediacy. In *Rabbit, Run*, however, the language seems stubbornly closed, almost irritating in its impoverishment. It remains puzzling and irritating until you relinquish certain expectations of the language—that it is a formal system requiring forward movement, and implying a logical progression from *here* to *there* within each sentence. The language of

Rabbit, Run is instead a vehicle of intuition, recognition, pattern, parable, and omen. The key words are smooth as mantras, narrow sounds snapped free of context, pure objects of contemplation, the stones that Rabbit touches again and again in his nervous circling. In the beginning of the novel these word-touchstones are "trap" and "net." "Run" remains a constant, as frequently invoked as in a primer, often rather hopefully, as if it were the verb particular to salvation. Near the middle of the novel, things are described as "tipped" or "tipping," until the entire physical universe seems precariously out-of-balance. In *Rabbit, Run* the world never rights itself. The novel ends, not with symmetry or release, exactly, but with a sigh that could be either exhaustion or sly physical pleasure in motion itself: "Ah: runs. Runs."

Women, rooms, the twigs of a forest, the straps of a whore's shoes, all can be "nets" for Rabbit:

> The clutter behind him in the room—the Old-fashioned glass with its corrupt dregs, the choked ashtray balanced on the easy-chair arm, the rumpled rug, the floppy stacks of slippery newspapers, the kid's toys here and there broken and stuck and jammed, a leg off a doll and a piece of bent cardboard that went with some breakfast-box cut-out, the rolls of fuzz under the radiators, the continual crisscrossing mess—clings to his back like a tightening net. (*Rabbit, Run*: 18)

> At the upper edge of his headlight beams the naked tree-twigs make the same net. Indeed the net seems thicker now. (*Rabbit, Run*: 37)

> The names melt away and he sees the map whole, a net, all those red lines and blue lines and stars, a net he is somewhere caught in. (*Rabbit, Run*: 39)

> He feels the faded night he left behind in this place as a net of telephone calls and hasty trips, trails of tears and strings of words, white worried threads shuttled through the night and now faded but still existent, an invisible net overlaying the steep streets and in whose center he lies secure in his locked hollow hutch. (*Rabbit, Run*: 43)

In this last passage, "white worried threads shuttled through the night" is an oblique reference to Rabbit's wife, whom he has earlier remembered as "just a girl. Nerves like new thread. Skin smelled like fresh cotton." (*Rabbit, Run*: 18) Thread can be woven into nets; even physiologically, she possesses the ability to trap him. Entrapment is a fact of their life—she trapped by pregnancy, he trapped into marriage—and an aspect of the world they share, where ashtrays are choked and toys are "broken and stuck and jammed."

> Janice calls from the kitchen. "And honey pick up a pack of cigarettes, could you?" in a normal voice that says everything is forgiven, everything is the same.
>
> Rabbit freezes, standing looking at his faint yellow shadow on the white door that leads to the hall, and senses he is in a trap. It seems certain. He goes out. (*Rabbit, Run*: 20)

> He doesn't drive five miles before this road begins to feel like a part of the same trap. (*Rabbit, Run*: 29)

This incantatory play of language is essential to *Rabbit, Run*, for it reflects and, in part, sustains the larger exigencies of the narrative—the passage of time, the whittling-away of freedom, the constant underlying sense of dread that Rabbit feels. The chronology of the novel is framed by a pair of events, the vernal equinox and the summer solstice, that were crucial in the ceremonial lives of primitive peoples, reverently observed by them as indications of consistency in the workings of the universe, *knowns* in the flux of time; they were also ways of pinning down the cycles of planting and harvest on which culture was dependent, of locating yourself between the broad horizons of spring and winter. The universe mirrored the trustworthiness of gods through the regular occurence of solstices and equinoxes, and their inviolate mystery through the chicanery of planets, which act according to no readily decipherable law. Without a formal and rather scrupulous knowledge of such events, only hunting and gathering was possible—you were forced to rely on the whims of abundance and scarcity with which the earth alternately presented you. The days for the planting of various crops, each according to the length of its growing span, were calculated from the vernal equinox, while those until harvest were counted from the summer solstice, making it a time of intense concentration, and often of fasting, the ceremonial sequestering of priests or shamans, and sacrifice. It is a procedure that Rabbit will echo with a curious precision in mourning for his daughter. The narrative seems to stem from these events—equinox and solstice—almost as much as it flows between them.

> Now, just a few minutes after six a day before the vernal equinox, all the houses and the gravel-roofed factories and the diagonal hillside streets are in the shadow that washes deep into the valley of farmland east of the mountain. (*Rabbit, Run*: 23)

> [Rabbit's] feeling that there is an unseen world is instinctive, and more of his actions than anyone suspects constitute transactions with it. He dresses in his new gray suit and steps out at a quarter of eleven into a broad blue Sunday morning a day before the summer solstice. (*Rabbit, Run*: 217)

The way in which each mention of the day and hour is fitted into the text hardly seems accidental; each is "a day before," although one deals in a preoccupied way with an enormous shadow, and the other with a "broad blue" morning light. The equinox is associated with a shadow that "washes deep into the valley of farmland," mimicking, at least to my ear, "Yea, though I walk through the valley of the shadow of death." In the second instance, the solstice is tied to a description of Rabbit's transactions with an unseen world. It seems to me somewhat oddly phrased, for who exactly is the "anyone" failing to suspect the belief behind Rabbit's actions? Does "anyone" mean the people near Rabbit, who are admittedly baffled by his behavior, or does it imply the reader of the novel, another, vaguer "anyone" existing on the periphery of Rabbit's world? Updike does have a way sometimes of turning unexpectedly from the fiction and poking his finger, whimsically or reprovingly, at the reader—as he did in the aphorisms of *Couples*. "And I find," he has said, "I can not imagine being a writer without wanting somehow to play, to make these patterns, to insert these secrets into my books, to spin out this music that has its formal side." (*Picked-Up Pieces*: 481) It seems implied that *we*, at least, should suspect the basis for Rabbit's actions, his sense of a pact struck with an unseen world, or he appears far more intransigent and shallow than he really is, and would scarcely deserve a second glance.

Neither is it, I think, absurdly farfetched to see Rabbit in a priestly guise, yet another variation of the pilgrim-hero, this time with a rather more substantial aura of saintliness. Eccles, the minister, rebukes Rabbit by saying "saints shouldn't marry," and teases him that, "flexible time. That's what you want, isn't it? Flexibility? So you can be free to preach to the multitudes?" (*Rabbit, Run*: 121) "Oh all the *world* loves you," Ruth, the prostitute with whom he briefly lives, tells Rabbit. "What I wonder is why?" (*Rabbit, Run*: 135) The stress is exact, on *world*, confirming Rabbit's connection with the "unseen world," the encompassing cosmos whose signals are ignored by everyone but him. Why shouldn't the world love him? In a long list of the names of songs and sorts of commercials that Rabbit hears on his car's radio the first time he abandons his wife and really runs, it is mentioned that "the whereabouts of the Dalai Lama, spiritual leader of this remote and backward land, are unknown." (*Rabbit, Run*: 34) The paragraph concludes with a mocking lilt: "Where is the Dalai Lama?" (*ibid.*) Clearly, it is Rabbit whose whereabouts are unknown; the "remote and backward land" of which he is the spiritual leader is that chaotic apartment he inhabits with his resentful wife, Janice, who is well into her second pregnancy. This identification between Rabbit and the missing Dalai Lama is subsequently strengthened:

> [Rabbit] feels freedom like oxygen everywhere around him; Tothero is an eddy of air, and the building he is in, the streets of the town, are mere stairways and alley-ways in space. So perfect, so consistent is the freedom into which the clutter of the world has been vaporized by the simple trigger of his decision, that all ways seem equally good, all movements will put the same caressing pressure on his skin, and not an atom of his happiness would be altered if Tothero told him they were not going to meet two girls but two goats, and they were going not to Brewer but to Tibet. He adjusts his necktie with infinite attention, as if the little lines of this juncture of the Windsor knot, the collar of Tothero's shirt, and the base of his own throat were the arms of a star that will, when he is finished, extend outward to the rim of the universe. *He* is the Dalai Lama. (*Rabbit, Run*: 51-52)

Tothero (Tot/hero) was Rabbit's coach while he was a star basketball player, and serves as a sort of priestly mentor, whose shirt Rabbit literally wears. The paragraph is a little treatise on Tao, "that in virtue of which all things happen or exist," and under whose sway "all ways seem equally good," and the correct behavior is inspired by the moment, free of value judgements, unencumbered by social rigidities. For Rabbit, this perfect and unblinking recognition of Tao will be fairly frequent—in a sense, he is a man addicted to the seeking of *satori*, but ignorant of the codices and rituals that are meant to lend shape and dignity to such seeking. And, although frequent, these recogitions are fleeting. Rabbit customarily cares about the difference between girls and goats, and feels that both oxygen and freedom are rare commodities. But Brewer *is* his Tibet, his realm, circumscribed and impoverished; if he lacks the contemplativeness of a Dalai Lama, at least his presence seems, curiously often, to inspire love.

Rabbit will tend the world in more than the dainty adjustment of a necktie's knot. After his escape from Janice, while he is living with Ruth, he alters the way she lives, confines her for a time to housewifely things, cooking, the reading of paperback mysteries—in short, in almost Christ-like fashion, he renders a prostitute virtuous, and salvages from the disorder of her life something of affection and purpose. In the habit of Updike's heroes, he makes her, almost immediately, his wife.

> She tries to twist away, but now he holds the arm he touched. She says, "Say, do you think we're married or something the way you boss me around?"
>
> The transparent wave moves over him again and he calls to her in a voice that is almost inaudible, "Yes; let's be." So quickly her arms don't move from hanging at her sides, he kneels at her feet and kisses the place on her finger where a ring would have been. (*Rabbit, Run*: 75)

"I made you," he tells her. "I made you and the sun and the stars . . . I made you bloom." His passion cuts against her barrenness. He insists, the first time they make love, that she be absolutely naked, naked as Eve, and—without her diaphragm—

as defenseless. So Rabbit returns her to a woman's original functions, obedience and procreation, as chronicled in the admonitory tone of Genesis: "in pain you shall bring forth children, yet your desire shall be for your husband, and he shall rule over you." Her desire *is* for Rabbit. Makeshift husband that he is, and clumsily importunate Adam, he restores to her not only an aboriginal nakedness but also her own capcity for orgasm:

> "I had forgotten," she says.
> "Forgot what?"
> "That I could have it too."
> "What's it like?"
> "Oh. It's like falling through."
> "Where do you fall to?"
> "Nowhere. I can't talk about it." (*Rabbit, Run*: 83)

Updike's Adams and Eves are often inarticulate with each other, but in this case the distance between them, the ability to talk, is profound.

While Rabbit is living with Ruth, the work that he finds is among other, literal blooms, for he goes to work in the garden of an old woman, Mrs. Smith, whose dead husband's consuming passion was for rhododendrons. The passages that deal with Rabbit's work in the garden carry a shy freight of happiness, and in their gorgeousness, they come to seem a kind of paen to richness, fecundity, and order.

> Sun and moon, sun and moon, time goes. In Mrs. Smith's acres, crocuses break the crust. Daffodils and narcissi unpack their trumpets. The reviving grass harbors violets, and the lawn is suddenly coarse with dandelions and broad-leaved weeds. Invisible rivulets running brokenly make the low land of the estate sing. The flowerbeds,

bordered with bricks buried diagonally, are pierced by dull red spikes that will be peonies, and the earth itself, scumbled, horny, raggedly patched with damp and dry, looks like the oldest and smells like the newest thing under Heaven. (*Rabbit, Run*: 127)

"Funny, for these two months he never has to cut his fingernails," the following paragraph begins. Rabbit is bringing these things forth by the sweat of his brow. When he plants the packets of seeds that the old woman gives him, he "loves folding the hoed ridge of soil over the seeds. Sealed, they cease to be his. The simplicity. Getting rid of something by giving it to itself." It is an equation even more ancient than Genesis, this metaphor in which the planting of seeds is linked to the insemination of a woman. Rabbit seems, for once, truly stable, dutiful, and at ease—all within the boundaries of the garden.

I would like to double back for a time to the peculiarities of the opening pages of the novel, because they contain further clues to Rabbit's character and fate; not only the language, but the dramatic stop-and-go movement of the narration, constructs a pattern for what will follow. These pages can be examined in grave detail, because they are very nearly as tightly coded and neatly interlocking as the sequences of rhyme in a sonnet. The dialogue bristles with omens. The very first word that Rabbit, hero of a trilogy that has spanned three decades so far, ever says is "Hey!" a shout of exaltation following a successful free throw (he has intruded into a boy's game in an alley, after the basketball thumps to his feet). *Rabbit, Run* opens with this hosannah, a cry of prideful greeting, and slips away from it, never to return to exactly this pitch of unthinking grace where luck and skill intersect.

None of this is casual, although Updike's use of the present tense (he has called it "a mild adventure") renders the prose random-looking and quick. Free throws are granted to players who have been fouled, and Rabbit's life has been fouled, not in any technical sense, but in the meaning of having been obscurely dirtied at its source, diminished in purity. How this happens is not exactly clear, even to Rabbit; he only knows that it *has* happened, that his course has been a falling-off from a brief and original grace. He was once a basketball player, locally famous, so agile he could score twenty-three points in the first game he played. With his second word, the matter-of-factly inflected "Skill," Rabbit attempts to regain his old footing of nobility, for he was that most wonderful of heroes, a "natural," a "young deer," as Tothero calls him, who needed only the most rudimentary instruction to reach excellence. This initial metaphor, locked in place with the first exchange of dialogue between Rabbit and the boys, is one that will haunt Rabbit throughout his life. So neatly, so inevitably, did he once embody the metaphor—athletic prowess manifesting grace of spirit—that he rarely troubles to move beyond it. He believes that the graceful is the good; he only wishes to be good again.

Just after "Skill," Rabbit says, "Ok if I play?" The reader understands that this question—unpunctuated, off-handed plea that it is—will lie just below the surfaces of Rabbit's life, consuming his attention, for play is sexual as well as athletic, and the ingratiating "Ok" is Rabbit's ticket, a sort of open-sesame he will apply to women, to the world, as well as to young boys playing basketball in a Brewer alley.

It is odd, too, that in a series of novels whose hero will be so adamantly alert to sexual possibility—constantly speculating about other men's wives, rich women, poor women, women on the street, finally even, in *Rabbit Is Rich*, his own daughter-in-law—that the very first sexual imagery in *Rabbit, Run* is homosexual, occurring in the book's second paragraph: "The cigarette makes it more sinister still. Is this one going to offer them cigarettes or money to go out in back of the ice plant with him? They've heard of such things but are not too frightened; there are six of them and one of him." (*Rabbit, Run*: 9)

87

Throughout the novel the ice plant will be an ominous symbol, a kind of fixed locale for iciness and evil:

> At the next corner, where the water from the ice plant used to come down, sob into a drain, and reappear on the other side of the street, Rabbit crosses over and walks beside the gutter where the water used to run, coating the shallow side of its course with ribbons of green slime waving and waiting to slip under your feet and dunk you if you dared walk on them. He can remember falling in but not why he was walking along this slippery edge in the first place. (*Rabbit, Run*: 20)

Rabbit is trapped at the level of a fairy tale, bogged down by an immense weight of detail, memories of "falling in." One of the things he has fallen into is marriage. He and Janice were caught in the classic way, by pregnancy, but their knowledge of why they were "walking along this slippery edge in the first place" is negligible. The first thing that she ever says, in the novel, is "It just locked itself." She is speaking of the door to their apartment, but the comment is so numbingly appropriate to Janice, the intensity with which she creates and then shuts herself into chaos, that Rabbit bewilderedly repeats: "Just locked itself." Within moments they are arguing:

> "You're supposed to look tired. You're a modern housewife."
>
> "And meanwhile you're off in the alley playing like a twelve-year-old?"
>
> It gripes him that she didn't see his crack about being a housewife, based on the "image" the MagiPeel people tried to have their salesmen sell to, as ironical and at bottom pitying and fond. There seems no escaping it; she is dumb. He says, "Well what's the difference if you're sitting here watching a program for kids under two?"

> "Who was *shushing* a while ago?"
>
> "Ah, Janice." He sighs. "Screw you. Just screw you."
> (*Rabbit, Run*: 17)

In this exchange they exhaust each other's limited resources—for gentleness, rue, companionability—with the abbreviated hostility of two people who consider each other so predictable that even a fight will yield nothing new. In fact, they know each other in ways that are almost unendurable. Rabbit is right to feel, as he does, somewhat frightened of Janice; in her haphazard depression she is a frightening woman. She is right to resent his vagrancy, for it threatens the little that they have. She detects his momentary freedom, and it throws her confinement into sharper relief. From her position, even aimlessness seems a gift. Saints shouldn't marry; if they do, their wives are in trouble.

> Janice calls from the kitchen. "And honey pick up a pack of cigarettes, could you?" in a normal voice that says everything is forgiven, everything is the same.
>
> Rabbit freezes, standing looking at his faint yellow shadow on the white door that leads into the hall, and senses he is in a trap. It seems certain. He goes out. (*Rabbit, Run*: 19-20)

This matching of "everything is forgiven" with "everything is the same" is the basis of Rabbit's terror, for in a world so shadowed with Christian nuance forgiveness ought to alter, to divest and purge the sameness from things; it ought to be a kind of lever by which things are forced to a newer, finer plane. Instead, this contradiction, hinged by something as slim as a comma, causes Rabbit to confront his shadow for the first time in the book. He knows that such sameness is a kind of dying, and that her forgiveness is simply a means by which he is nudged closer to his own death. Like the hero of the short story "Leaves" who basks in an epiphany in the form of light falling flat across the floor, "like a penitent," Rabbit is forced into awareness by the sight of this "faint yellow shadow." Shadows and light are often a mode of recognition in Updike's work. This instance is almost painterly in its exactitude, because Rabbit sees not only a faint shadow, but a faint yellow shadow on a white door, and yellow—at least in the jargon of gradeschool playgrounds, a language not at all alien to Updike's imagination, nor, one assumes, to Rabbit's—is the color of cowardice, retreat from battle, and flight.

Even so, Rabbit's response fails immediately to crystallize. He thinks only that "it seems certain." In nearly everything, Rabbit shies from any too-definite architecture of response; that would be simply one more way of locking himself in. It is almost difficult to imagine any circumstances in which Rabbit could be found thinking to himself, "It is absolutely certain." He is responsive, above all, to apprehension, the emotion you have when things *seem* dangerous or unpredictable. The physical environment of Brewer fosters this state of mind, for it is queerly numinous, in its kitchens, windows, alleys, and eaves, factories and flights of stairs, ice plants and cathedrals. How deftly Updike constructs a sacred wood:

> Outdoors it is growing dark and cool. The Norway maples exhale the smell of their sticky new buds and the broad living-room windows along Wilbur Street show beyond the silver patch of a television set the warm bulbs burning in kitchens, like fires at the backs of caves. He walks downhill. The day is gathering itself in. He now and then touches with his hand the rough bark of a tree or the dry twigs of a hedge, to give himself the small answer of a texture. At the corner, where Wilbur Street meets Potter Avenue, a mailbox stands leaning in twilight on its concrete post. Tall two-petalled street sign, the cleat-gouged trunk of the telephone pole holding its insulators against the sky, fire hydrant like a golden bush: a grove.
> (*Rabbit, Run*: 20)

Like any hero just setting out on his journey, Rabbit must feel partly enthralled and partly fearful, because this world is so visibly enchanted. The world in *Rabbit, Run* must be numinous to reflect Rabbit's conflicting emotions and tangled potential—maples must "breathe," telephone wires "sing," the insulators be "giant blue eggs in a windy nest," in order to show Rabbit himself as a pilgrim-saint, a hero in disguise. While the physical environment of Brewer often seems too crushingly narrow for adults, Rabbit remains queerly child-like, at least if vulnerability and inventiveness are child-like qualitites. In a crucial sense, he is still willing to play, to seem to be what he is not, to daydream a new life for himself and then move in to fill its perimeters. He is credulous. At the deepest level of interpretation, Rabbit is the best believer of any of Updike's various heroes, and the kingdom—perhaps eventually that of Heaven, but for now the wide and changeable kingdom of the earth—is his.

the end

Sources

John Updike

Assorted Prose (New York: Fawcett World Library, 1966)

Bech: A Book (New York: Vintage, 1980)

The Centaur (New York: Fawcett Crest, 1964)

Couples (New York: Fawcett Crest, 1969)

Marry Me: A Romance (New York: Fawcett Crest, 1976)

Museums and Women (New York: Alfred A. Knopf, 1972)

The Music School (New York: Vintage, 1980)

Of the Farm (New York: Fawcett Crest, 1965)

Picked-Up Pieces (New York: Fawcett Crest, 1975)

The Poorhouse Fair (New York: Alfred A. Knopf, 1958)

Problems and Other Stories (New York: Alfred A. Knopf, 1979)

Rabbit Is Rich (New York: Alfred A. Knopf, 1981)

Rabbit Run (New York: Fawcett Crest, 1962)

Too Far to Go (New York: Fawcett Crest, 1979)

John Callaway

John Callaway Interviews John Updike (Kent: P.T.V. Publications, 1981)

Biographical notes: Elizabeth Tallent was born in Washington, D.C. in 1954. Her fiction has appeared in the *New Yorker*; one story was included in *The Best American Short Stories of 1981*. A collection of her short stories, *In Constant Flight*, will be published by Alfred A. Knopf. She now lives in Eaton, Colorado.